P9-CRY-599

WAR JOURNAL OF AN INNOCENT SOLDIER

The GI directly below me was hit dead center. It was our platoon runner, formerly a cook. He couldn't get up so he began yelling for help. He knew I was somewhere nearby so he yelled for me occasionally and for Woody Powers, who'd had his scalp creased by a bullet on Mt. Belvedere. Woody didn't show up to help, and I knew I wouldn't either. Heroes are supermen who apparently have no fear. I could not overcome mine.

"I'm hit in the stomach!" he yelled. "Help! . . . Help! . . . Don't leave me to die! Medic! . . . Medic! . . ." Silence. And then he started all over again. I could hear his cries weaken. We hadn't seen a medic all afternoon.

After a while the runner stopped yelling.

"Like an infantry patrol—sharp-eyed, tense, and close to the ground . . . A fine book"

Samuel Hynes, Professor of Literature
at Princeton University, author of
Flights of Passage

WAR JOURNAL OF AN
INNOCENT SOLDIER

JOHN T. BASSETT

AVON BOOKS ◆ NEW YORK

AVON BOOKS
A division of
The Hearst Corporation
105 Madison Avenue
New York, New York 10016

The Archon Books edition contains the following Library of Congress
Cataloging in Publication Data:

Bassett, John T.
    The war journal of an innocent soldier / John T. Bassett.
    p. cm.
    1. Bassett, John T.   2. World War, 1939–1945—Personal narratives,
American.   3. World War, 1939–1945—Italy.   I. Title.
D811.B3619   1989
940.54′8173—dc20   89-14973   CIP

First Avon Books Printing: January 1991

This Journal is dedicated to Hester Bassett, without whose understanding none of the following would have been possible.

Drummer Hodge

I

They throw in Drummer Hodge to rest
  Uncoffined—just as found:
His landmark is a kopje-crest
  That breaks the veldt around;
And foreign constellations West
  Each night above his mound.

II

Young Hodge the Drummer never knew—
  Fresh from his Wessex home—
The meaning of the broad Karoo,
  The Bush, the dusty loam,
And why uprose to nightly view
  Strange stars amid the gloam.

III

Yet portion of that unknown plain
  Will Hodge forever be;
His homely Northern breast and brain
  Grow to some Southern tree,
And strange-eyed constellations reign
  His stars eternally.

Thomas Hardy

April 14, 1945

THE MORNING DAWNED BRIGHT AND CLEAR. THIS morning we were to begin our last offensive action against Kesselring's northern Italy stronghold in the Appenines, approximately twenty miles south of Bologna. For many days we had been sweating this out on our Italian hillside, sitting in the warm spring sunshine by our foxholes. We had little to do except write letters home, stand guard, and wonder when it would begin. At night we would gather in a central area, sit on the ground, and, in total darkness, sing and tell stories. When one of us was killed, the memory was etched for the rest of our lives inside us in a terrible unique way.

And now the hour was upon us. The cooks, as usual, would stay behind and carry ammunition and come up later to the front in jeeps if the offensive was successful. Each man now picked up his supply of ammo and grenades. We put the heavy bandoliers around our necks. Each man was issued three boxes of K rations. We stripped them down to reduce their bulk and stuffed the parcels into our pockets.

H hour was 9:15 A.M. We ate our last hot meal on the hillside and watched the company chaplain perform Mass on the hood of his jeep for some Catholic soldiers. Several non-Catholic GIs walked down to

1

the outer fringe of the kneeling soldiers and also kneeled down, removed their helmets and clasped their hands together against their chests. The large ornate altar cloth, snowy white, caught and held my eye and made me wonder if this last brief service was nothing more than last rites being administered to doomed men—killers, prisoners—about to be executed. The fear of death—of dying—was everywhere among us and within us. Our thoughts ceased, our faces grew taut and white with dread expectation.

Fifteen minutes before H hour, our artillery began a terrific barrage to soften the enemy up. Heavy mortars, the 105s, 75s, the 155s, and even the tanks opened up. The noise was deafening. Shells whistled over our heads, screaming and churning the cool morning air into a lather of molten steel. Just before it ended we were assembled by platoon to hear our orders. My company (I Company) would lead the way, and my platoon (3rd Platoon), would be second in the order of march. Here and there men called out a last farewell. There was no laughter.

Captain Bucher motioned us forward silently and we went over the brow of the hill. A five yard interval was taken between men. Just below us on the reverse slope a large mulepack train was assembled to bring us food and water that night. Going over the crest of the hill, we could see where our shells were landing. Beyond the quarter mile of field stretching in front of us clouds of white smoke were bursting all over several wooded hills.

Now we started to half-trot, half-run across the field, stumbling and panting furiously under the extra weight of ammo and grenades. Our faces grew red and hot and our legs became weak from the killing pace and from fear. Sergeant John Holman, our squad leader, who resembled Gary Cooper in his youth, kept yelling back for us to hurry and catch up with him. But the shell fire was too loud. Some of the stragglers couldn't hear him, nor I when I yelled back also. When one fell behind, the whole column behind him automatically slowed down. And they weren't in the habit of passing each other. Directly ahead now was a barren slope that had to be climbed in order to gain our first objective, a wooded hill which was directly beyond. Here, before the hill, we hesitated. We were uncertain, and filled with inertia. We had crossed the field in ten minutes; now I found I was stripped of my strength. Had I run five miles already? Where was my stamina? I was twenty years old, and in great physical condition. My legs kept saying: You'll never make it up this hill. But my will to go on was greater. My will said: You've got to keep up, you can't fall behind now—think what they would say if you fell out now—keep going—keep going!

So I kept going and on the other side the knoll fell away steeply into a ravine. We scrambled into the creek bed only to be confronted with another steep wooded slope. It was so steep that progress was made only by pulling ourselves slowly upward from tree to tree. Was not this a struggle in futility, I asked myself? Was it not all useless—but I moved on. The sounds that beat into my ears had changed: our artillery units had stopped firing; now I just heard the heavy machine guns drilling away from their strategic positions behind us at the Krauts. Halfway up the hill, we were stopped by enemy artillery and machine gun fire. We were so exhausted that no one moved or attempted to dig in. More shells came screaming in and one hit somewhere above me, killing two and wounding one. We needed no more urging: I yanked my shovel out of my belt and started a slit trench as fast as I could dig. I heard another shell coming in and it sounded like it was going to be a direct hit on me. I clawed at the ground, held my breath and waited. It came in with a hellish whistle and exploded about fifty feet below me. The sound of the shrapnel ripping into the trees was terrifying. It slashed and cut through the leaves and flew into the ground everywhere. I turned and saw a big cloud of black smoke rising from the ground through the trees. Oh God, but that was close! But I could not marvel at not being hit because there came Fuller crawling up toward me, bug-eyed and miraculously unhurt; he'd been even closer than I.

"We've got to get out of here!" he gasped. "This is no fucking good!" But I could not move without an order from Sgt. Holman or Captain Bucher, so I fell to digging my hole feverishly again. All around me others were doing the same thing—some methodically, some furiously, some despairingly. A few were too tired or they had lost their shovels. Is this not hopeless, I thought? Will I die a horrible death? But I kept digging in spite of my despairing thoughts and managed to scoop out a hole that would partially protect me from bullets and shrapnel, but not from a tree burst. The mortar section came staggering up through us; they were able to do very little under all those trees.

I was dry as a bone and sweating like a horse, so I threw off my jacket, my bandoliers and my grenades and drank a little from my canteen. I wondered how long it would last. Why did I think about water now? Was it a precious as my life? Would it keep me safe? Maybe not, but it would keep me digging until . . . A little more time lapsed and I kept digging. A GI came to me suddenly and tried to squeeze in the hole with me when a couple of shells hit nearby, but he only succeeded in covering me up good. After that he helped me dig.

Then, above me, near a stone wall, Holman signalled for us to get ready to move. I threw on my equipment and waited for another signal. He motioned again and we started towards him. At the stone wall we knelt down while he gave us some instructions. There was a small field to our right. We were to run across it, keeping ten yards between us. Upon reaching a path beyond the field we were to stop and take cover by the stone wall and await further orders. We nodded that we understood and started off. It was a short distance and I made it easily and fell on my stomach on the path already thickly filled with men. Sgt. Penny our new 1st Sergeant who replaced Schnitzler who ran away one night after a heavy mortar bombardment and lost all I company's records lay calmly on one side of me and Holman lay on the other side. Holman lay very still with his eyes shut. He seemed to be trying to shrink inside his jacket. My jacket had become a burden so I took it off and left it on the path. Over on the path, a little to my left, Lt. Quam lay on his back. He had been hit by shrapnel only a few minutes ago, and was dead. His blue combat badge, pinned proudly to his shirt, shone in the bright sun. He looked stiff. He looked lifeless. Quam had been a new addition to our battalion. He was very young and eager to lead men into battle. Big black flies were swarming around his staring yellowish face. I turned so that I would not puke. A barrage of Kraut shells came in then and we all flattened ourselves against the wall. They hit all over the field beyond us and because the earth was soft the shells went

5

in far enough so that when they finally exploded the blasts went mostly straight up. So we lay unharmed. Then we stood up a couple of times and fired our M1s over the wall at a house beyond and above it. There were snipers there shooting at the men crossing the field. One man, almost to the path, was hit in the chest and fell to the ground. Twisting and squirming, he struggled with all his might to get up, but could not. Penny, Holman and I lay there and watched the pathetic sight. Was it not certain death to run out there and bring him to the wall? We certainly thought so, as did everyone else who saw it, except one man: Tech. Sgt. Carafa. Carafa, who had been lying by the wall, suddenly decided to help him, and after yelling for some covering fire, ran out to the wounded GI. A 2nd lieutenant ran out also and together they brought him back safely to the wall.

"Carafa Carafa Carafa—Carafa Carafa Carafa" his platoon would sing to some old ditty while swinging in to Camp Swift, Texas, from a long hot hike at dusk. His men loved him: they would do anything for him. He was a small brown Italian with a natural comic persona. He was flamboyant, he was a leader of men, and now I saw that he was an authentic hero.

We needed to get up and move out. This lying pinned down on an open path was the shits. Some more 88s came in and exploded in the field, and in the silence that followed I heard an unbelievable sound. Surely, I thought, I am hearing the song of an angel who has come down from heaven to save us all from this wicked war . . . No, my ears deceived me, but I heard a song. The lilting sweet carol of a skylark. It spiraled up and up into the clear blue sky, singing happily. I turned over on my side and searched the sky. At last I made it out, a tiny speck, way up high, circling round and round.

Lt. Robert Sabin, our platoon leader, suddenly stood up. Sabin was another young lieutenant, tall and thin with a prominent Adam's apple and an awkward smile that belied his intense dedication to the Army, and now he was beginning to assert himself, his way. He told us to cover him while he went ahead to find out the story, the reason for the big delay. Luhaink, my good Polish buddy from Massachusetts, and I crawled to where we could see up the path as he went. We gave this up in a minute because he was soon out of sight so we just huddled together beside the wall. It was very warm there in the sun. I wondered: should I throw my jacket over Lt. Quam's face? It was just an extra weight for me, and besides, it would be a decent thing to do. Goddamn those black flies: they were bothering us now. They clung to my skin like sticky fingers. But I decided against it: my jacket was somewhere behind me, out of sight, so why take an unnecessary chance. Anyway, he was dead. It was just the way his face looked.

The day was going rapidly now; already it was 3:30 in the afternoon. If somebody didn't do something, we might never take our objective. Then again, maybe that wouldn't be so bad. The white dirt road winding back through the fields looked terribly inviting, and we could see prisoners and walking wounded going back. The war for them was over: no more fighting, no more sweat and no more fear!

"Hey! Watch it will ya!" Joe Yerchin admonished me. My legs were pushing his BAR muzzle a little in the dirt. Getting dirt in your barrel was no fun. If the gun blew up, you were left defenseless or badly hurt. Either way it was no good. Word finally came around

7

the wall for our platoon to move forward down the path. Don't bunch up if you can help it, and keep low, we were cautioned. Slowly, carefully, we worked our way through the other GIs sprawled on the path, some of whom were now attempting to dig holes in the path. Another fifteen minutes delay and then we were again moving out along the path. Some 88s came in and we all hit the ground in a hurry. Some were exploding above the path and some below. In either case they were too close. The shrapnel will get my legs or my feet, at least, I thought. Got to protect them—draw them up close, turn over and lie on them. I pushed up tight against the bank. It's no good to keep going, it's all fucked up, it's crazy, but what the hell can I do? Just move along when they tell me to. The line moved again and I with it. When I was moving, I couldn't move fast enough and I cursed when we slowed down. As long as we were moving, I felt safe from being hit. It didn't matter where we were going either. I was just going somewhere with my squad. I was moving with a group of men. There was a feeling of security that came from being close to them. Here and there a man would never rise again to move in the line. So it was; while most of us went forward, there were some who stayed behind.

Ahead we saw four Krauts coming along the path carrying one of their wounded on an improvised stretcher. Some of the men were calling them names. As they passed us I noticed how well fitted they were in their rich green uniforms. They were young and well fed, but very frightened. Lt. Sabin was a very brave man; once again he was telling us to stay put while he went ahead to see what the holdup was. Our objective was closer, but there was still an open field to run across and it was going to be all uphill. Sabin reappeared. "Come on! Let's go!" he yelled, "the line's moving again. Keep ten yards when you cross this field . . . pass it back!" And the instructions were passed back along the line. The field was very steep. I saw Holman start running up the path. But he finished walking. I started across, running as fast as I could. I wanted to run every step of the way, but I couldn't do it. My wind gave out and I too slowed to a walk. An 88 came in pretty close and we all fell flat. Shells, shells . . . always with you.

I fell down on my side and waited for an order, or a sign from Sabin or Holman. We were now at the fringe of the wooded ridge; our objective must be near. I looked around and then I saw Brown crawling up to me. Brown was a small soldier. He came from Pittsburgh, where the steel mills were. He had worked in the mills. He worked with men who spoke Italian and he picked up their language. In the small mountain village of Prunetta, where we were billeted in January, Brown talked to an old Italian who had worked in the steel mills of Pittsburgh in 1919. I was impressed that they could talk to each other: the old small Italian, and the young small American, using poor Italian and poor English to find they had worked in the same industry in America. They had finally broken into smiles and clapped each others' shoulders before parting. Brown crept up to me.

"Bass," he said, looking at me from under his steel helmet, his white face smeared with dirt.

"Yeah—what is it, Brown?" I said.

"Bass, I've gotta go back. I can't take any more."

"What do you mean?" I said, shocked at his words.

"I've had all I can take. I'm going back. Tell Holman I talked to you, will you?" He began to slide back away from me.

"Wait!" I cried.

"No," he said, "I'll go back with the walking wounded. I'll find the way. This is no good. I can't take any more. Goodbye, Bass."

He crawled back down the slope, and was gone. I never heard about Brown again. The little man from Pittsburgh, a gentle, quiet little man, had had enough of war. He could not stomach it. He could not find the strength to obey an order that might lead to his death. But he could face up to the blazing heat from the furnaces at Pittsburgh—that was honest heat—that was predictable. But this hillside with war rolling over it was not. Brown crept away, and I reacted righteously: OK, you goddamned little coward, I thought, I'm as scared as you, but I won't run away. No, I've never dropped out, I've never run away—not yet, anyway. You go, little scared man, I'll stay!

I quickly put Brown out of my mind and turned to the matter of continued survival for myself. This Italian hillside was not like the one we had left in the morning. The enemy was here, entrenched in caves, sitting in trees with sniper rifles, sending out round after round of 88mm shellfire, plus devastating mortar fire. It was traditional warfare. There were no air attacks. It was old traditional war that brought the German army and us together.

We got up in a few minutes and started for the top of the hill. It was slow work. The Krauts were firing all the time so we had to crawl on our stomachs. Sabin kept urging us on, "Come on, keep working up on them. If we can get their heads down, we've got 'em!" I could hear a machine gun ahead, hidden among the trees. But we gradually froze. Sabin saw this and yelled at two GIs with grenade launchers on their rifles.

"Hey! you two: fire some grenades over there!" The men he designated put grenades on their launchers and then carefully fired them through the trees. I heard only one small explosion. The machine gun nest was not affected.

"Come on! Come on! Let's go!" Sabin yelled. "Don't stop now, keep moving . . . you on the right there—let's go!" He was almost pleading with us now. Sgt. Johnson, calm and confident, was the farthest forward. He turned around frequently to see where we were. Now we had to be careful we did not shoot one of our men. The Krauts had a fine concealed position in those trees and they obviously weren't going to abandon it. Then we saw two men coming toward us from up front: one was holding his wrist. Blood dripped steadily from it. He was a little pale but he seemed happy to have got off so easily. The other had been hit in the leg. Those lucky dogs, I thought; they don't have to take this any more. Wouldn't it be worth it to get a nick in the arm or leg? God, but I'd have to be lucky. No, I won't wish any such thing. God! I just want to get through, I want to live through it so I can go home again!

Directly behind us was another wooded hill, smaller than ours. Near the crest were a row of dugouts covered with trees and leaves. Pfc. Rabideaux and others begin to get suspicious of them: "Hey!" he cried, "Let's find out if anyone's in them!" We agreed, and began firing. This went on for several minutes. Then, in one, we saw something moving. Two Krauts came out cautiously waving a white rag on a long branch. We all yelled up and down our hill to hold the fire. Dead prisoners was not policy. There

11

was an ugly rumor about that Sgt. Meier had lined up several Krauts on Mt. Belvedere at the edge of a sheer drop-off, and then shot them in a fit of rage with one of their own burp guns. They had all disappeared over the edge of the mountain. I believed the story because I knew a little about Meier. It was only his face that I knew: it was long, narrow and white and his eyes were set close together and they leered out at the world and in this war he found sufficient reason to kill, both in the heat of battle, and in the cold aftermath. But Luca Luhaink, my foxhole buddy, had almost done the same thing. After Mt. Belvedere was taken, we walked up on a large pile of frozen American corpses that had been gathered for identification and future burial. A single Kraut stood nearby with his hands clasped tight over his black helmet. Luhaink suddenly stepped towards him with his M1 thrust out—"See! See! You goddamned Kraut, what you did?" It was close. We grabbed Luhaink and pushed up the gun. He was very mad, but allowed us to bring him back to his senses in time.

We were worried about the snipers to our rear. We were really in a mess now. No one was moving forward anymore. We were turned around, facing a new danger from our rear.

"What time is it, Rabideaux?" I wanted to know.

"About four thirty."

"Why the hell don't they call this thing off? It's going to be dark before long and then we'll be stuck here."

"I don't know and I'm too damned tired to care much either." Sgt. Pete Ware was hit in the foot by a sniper, and another GI was hit at the same time. It was time to spread out. We were getting confused: a machine gun nest to our front and hidden snipers to

12

our rear was no joke. It was a little too open where I was, so I got up to run to a better place. I ran two steps and a sniper shot at me. C-r-rack!! The bullet hit the dirt beside my right foot and a small cloud of dust rose as it whined away into the woods. I turned sharply to my left and dove headlong into a clump of bushes. That was too close.

"Hey Bassett? Don't let him get away with that!" Sabin yelled from somewhere.

"Christ!" I yelled back. "Where is he?"

Then I became enraged: there was no explaining it. I forgot fear temporarily. Foolishly . . . desperately, I turned around and tried to locate that sniper. I stood up and ran along the densely wooded hill, disregarding all caution. As I dived towards another bush, several shots whistled over my head. I curled up in the bush and knew I'd made a mistake. My anger faded. Oh-oh boy, I thought, you went too far—you're alone out here—better get out of here and get back to the others—fast! I crawled out of the bush and crawled another ten yards and then got up and ran back. But to where? What I wanted was a hole. Then I saw one. A GI was in it. There had to be room for me too. I ran to it and flopped down on my stomach above the hole. The GI lay on his stomach with his head buried in the dirt as far as he could push it. From the waist down his body was exposed to the air. The hole was much too small. That didn't matter though. If I could get my head down in that hole, I knew I could survive. A bullet in my ass or my legs would hurt and I would bleed a lot, but I could live through it. A bullet in the head was good-bye.

"I'm moving in fella," I said, "there's no place else to go."

"OK," he muttered, "but get in quick and lie still. He'll spot you if you move around."

I was afraid he would see me anyway. The fresh dirt all around the hole stood out like a sore thumb. But I had to take it. I'd recognized my companion; it was Bucklin, BAR man in the second platoon. The earth was loose so I cautiously tried bringing up my right foot to see if I could push out some of the dirt. It was nerve wracking. If the sniper saw me, there would be an end to it.

"You better just lie still," Bucklin advised. "He won't see you as long as you lie still." So I gave it up and waited.

About fifteen feet below us two men lay motionless in the grass. The sniper must have had an excellent scope. He wasn't close to us because when he fired the crack of his rifle was rather faint. The GI directly below me was hit dead center, the other scrambled to his feet and took off through the woods. It was our platoon runner, formerly a cook. He couldn't get up so he began yelling for help. His voice was loud and strong and he kept it up for a long time. He knew I was somewhere nearby so he yelled for me occasionally and for Woody Powers who'd had his scalp creased by a bullet on Mt. Belvedere. Woody didn't show up to help, and I knew I wouldn't either. Heroes are supermen who apparently have no fear. I could not overcome my fear of the hidden sniper.

"I'm hit in the stomach!" he yelled. "Help! . . . Help! . . . Don't leave me to die! Medic! . . . Medic. . . ." Silence. And then he started all over again. I could hear his cries weaken. We hadn't seen a medic all afternoon. I became panicky and almost made a run for it to another place, but Bucklin persuaded me not to. After a while the runner stopped yelling. Still, no one came to help him.

Slowly, ever so slowly the light waned while we lay still. One German sniper had about twenty-four men lying motionless on the ground. The machine gun was quiet now. There was not a sound on that hill. At length the sunset glow left the sky and a grayness filtered into the woods. Only a little longer now, I thought.

When it grew a bit darker, I heard movements around me. I pushed up and saw some GIs bent over digging foxholes. I stood up cautiously and waited. The sniper was through for the day. It was too dark to see. I saw Luhaink, Mathews, Fronk and others, all digging. Sgt. Holman was with them trying to locate the rest of us. Holman and I decided to dig together since we were both alone. The ground was barely visible. We began shoveling like mad. He had a shovel and I had a pick. It was back-breaking work. The ground was interwoven with tough roots and underneath them were boulders that resisted all our efforts to unearth them. So we dug around them as best as we could. Holman was so exhausted he had to stop shoveling after a little. I was nearly ready to quit myself but something kept me digging. The boulders stopped us. Holman found two thin trees and put them over the head of the hole. "I guess they'll help a little," he said. Now we began to get cold, and I'd thrown away my jacket and had no blanket.

But I was lucky to be with Holman: he took out his canteen. It was half-full. I had no water left in mine. We drank that up in short order. And he had a raincoat, but I knew he would not share that with me. We were hungry, so we each had a fruit bar, cheese, some hard biscuits, some soup powder and a stick of gum. It had never tasted good before, but that night it was delicious.

Except for the sounds of shovels and picks chomping and hacking away at the heartless earth, all was quiet. The hill had not been won the first day and we had expected a counter attack. Were the Germans retreating? We did not know, and I couldn't talk about it with Holman. After a little, he spoke: "I guess we better try and get some rest. We'll take turns sleeping: an hour on and an hour off."

"OK," I said, "You take the first hour if you want. I'm going to scout around for some logs. Here—give me your watch—if any shells come in I'll probably jump right on top of you."

So Holman lay down around a boulder and wrapped the raincoat around him, pulled it over his head and buttoned it up. I took the pick and began poking around in the bushes. Close by I found more little broken trees and dragged them back, but got a little lost.

"Where the hell am I?" I asked of the dark. "Whose hole is this? . . . That you Fronk? . . . where's my hole?"

"Over to your left a little, Bass . . . How're ya doing?"

"Damned if I know . . . but I'm still alive," I answered wearily.

"Are we getting any water tonight?"

"Yeah, some of the third squad's gone down to the CP, wherever it is. Going to bring up two five gallon cans. You thirsty?"

"Goddamned right!—ain't you?"

"A little."

I laid the trees across the hole and tried not to spill too much dirt on Holman's head. Two hours went by

16

and on my turn to sit up again the third squad came with the water.

"Hey over there," one of them whispered loudly, "Where's Holman? We've got the water."

"Right here—sleeping with me," I whispered back. "Give me the water. I'll put them right here and when he gets up for his watch, he'll give it out—OK?"

"Yeah."

Water at last. Two cans of the precious stuff. Sitting there in the hole with it, I felt richer than any king in the world. Very carefully I poured my canteen cup full and gulped it down. How wonderful it was to feel that wetness in my throat . . . the coolness of it on my lips . . . it was a drink I will never forget.

I worried then about shrapnel or bullets hitting the cans. What if the water all drained out? That couldn't happen! I put them on their flat sides in my half of the hole and tried not to worry about it anymore. Fronk came over for a cup and went right back. I sat on the cans and probed around for a small piece of cheese I'd left somewhere near the edge of the hole. Where . . . where was that dry stinking cheese? Ah, there it was . . . but not enough . . . not nearly enough. God, I was so hungry I'd have eaten fresh bark.

Christ! I was hearing a familiar sound. Our artillery was letting loose again—chasing the Krauts away. Kee-rist! I thought—I hope none of those shells fall short—like they did after we took Mt. Belvedere. I had lain on the ground outside my hole with my double socks pulled off, letting them dry in the sun, along with my poor feet, when I heard our 75mm unit just below us fire off a round. It made a weird sound and the shell fell short into our men about a thousand yards from me. Instantly I heard screams amid the cloud of black smoke that rose from the impact area.

Now I listened: there . . . they're brushing those treetops out front. How in the dark can they tell where to aim? Judas! They are moaning like old sick cats . . . farther, farther and . . . now! Ca-a-room! Ca-bam!! C-crr-ump!!! And they burst somewhere out in enemy territory in small white flashes. It looked like we had attained our objective after all. I sank down into our hole and did not know when sleep came and brought me peace.

April 15, 1945

I STARTED TO UNBUTTON THE RAINCOAT (HOLMAN did share it with me after all), but before I'd opened my eyes I knew it was morning again. I felt it. I just knew. How I hated to face the light and reality once more. Everything was strange: the splintered trees, and weary bowed men sticking their heads up here and there above the earth, peering wonderingly at each other.

"Better stay down: that sniper's probably still around."

Absently: "Yeah." We were eating our K rations when Captain Bucher came by.

"Be ready to move out at 7 A.M. Holman," and he kept going. I hated him with a sullen passive energy that I could not understand. He had disciplined me in Camp Swift after I ran away from a barracks cleaning detail and played the piano for the GIs on a Sunday afternoon at the service club. I don't know how he had hurt me—except that he had humiliated me.

"Where did you go on Sunday, Bassett?" he said.

"I went down to the service club and played the piano for their Sunday program."

"For that you're restricted to the company area for

one month—and now you will report to the mess hall for KP duty until otherwise notified.''

After we had taken Mt. Belvedere, Captain Bucher suddenly came to me one afternoon where I was crouched down beside my hole. "Hey—uh, Bassett."

"Yeah?—Sir," I answered, looking up at him with suspicion.

"I didn't know you came from Watkins Glen, New York." I noticed he was holding a letter in his hand.

"Yes, that's right."

"Do you remember the regattas that were held on Seneca Lake?"

"Yes."

"Well, I used to come over from Corning. I spent many a Sunday there, sailing." I hated him so I did not know what to say. He lifted up my letter to my mother and smiled a little, and went back up to the CP.

So much for his sailing on my lake. He could never understand a love I had had—for a building—the service club at Camp Swift, Texas. It was a large rambling building with a music room on the second floor. There was a neat crooked stairway that led up to it. Inside and to the left was a walnut-brown Knabe grand piano. My mother had taught me to play the piano early in my childhood. I had never seen a piano as beautiful as that one. It pulled me to it like a giant magnet. I would go into the room after evening chow. If I was lucky, I would be alone. I would sit down on the leather bench, look up at the mellow stand-up lamp, and then I'd start with Gershwin's Second Prelude, then Rhapsody in Blue, then Deep Purple, and on to Rachmaninoff and the long sad preludes. The hostess at the service club soon became familiar with my routine. She was tall, but walked with an easy

20

grace. Her eyes were grayish green, and her hair, sandy red, fell in soft waves to her shoulders. Sometimes she smiled at me. I knew she understood about my love for music. I would always smile back, and sometimes say "hi." The service club became my very secret, very private refuge. The hostess was a part of it, but she did not try to intrude, to divert me from my music. In a dumb, unknowing way, I sometimes thought I loved her.

One hot morning we hiked out of camp nine miles for a week's bivouac. At day's end I lay under the edge of my two-man tent and looked out at the dusty Texas landscape. It was hot, and I was discontented. Suddenly I sat up and put on my boots. An idea was forming in my brain, but I sat a little longer and waited. It was not quite dark when I scrambled to my feet. I knew what I was going to do: I was returning to camp to play the piano. It was quiet around the tent. I got up and stole away and went down the dusty white road back to Camp Swift. It was soon dark, and as I walked along, I gradually tilted my head back, my eyes fixed steadily on the stars, shimmering and winking a display that expanded and enriched my young and simple soul.

I reached Camp Swift and headed for the service club. The camp was deserted. I entered the service club and ran up the steps to the music room. Once in the room, I sat down at the piano. The lamp was lit. All was quiet. I began to play, better than ever before. After an hour of bliss, I knew it was time to leave. I drew my thumb across the white keys in a farewell glissando and left the room in a kind of trance. Music had recharged my soul in a way I had devised on a night filled with starlight, in the dark

21

dusty silence of an army camp in Texas in the summer of 1944.

Halfway across the main floor I saw the hostess heading me off. So I stopped.

"What are you doing here?"

"I came in to play the piano."

"How were you planning to get back?"

"Like I got here—just walk back." She looked at me. Her face was unsmiling. Her tone was even, but firm:

"No—I think I'll drive you back."

"Drive me back?"

"Yes, I can't see you walking back. It's late and you must be very tired."

"Well, OK, but I can do it really OK by myself."

"No, I insist on driving you back. Aren't you in I Company about a mile up Pershing Road?"

"Yes—but—"

"I'll meet you in front of your barracks in half an hour."

I could not believe my luck. I shouted a thank you to God and danced across the road and ran in circles and backwards in case she should start for me early. I arrived at the barracks and sat down under the street light to wait for her. God, I loved her so! I often walked the base at night when I was through playing the piano. Sometimes I saw her, in my mind's eye. And heard her soft Texas voice. The camp was so quiet I began to feel a little strange. Time inched along; and then I thought: she didn't mean it, but I love her anyway. She just doesn't remember: she doesn't remember what she said. I guess I'll get up pretty quick and head on back to bivouac. The street light shown down on me, and I leaned over in the grass and thought: "She will not come. Why would she do this for me?"

But then I saw headlights coming. I roused up and looked. They came steadily toward me. My heart beat faster. I said aloud: "God, she loves me—what shall I do?" The car slowed and turned in to me. It was a pickup truck. But she was not driving. I opened the door.

"Hi, Bassett. This is my husband, Joe."

I said a muffled hello. He nodded and looked at me briefly. She motioned for me to sit beside her. I climbed in and faced up to the truth that she was married and that this ride was an act of charity only. Her husband said nothing and she said nothing, and so of course, I remained silent. It was a long, dark nine miles back to the bivouac site. He was silent: I knew why. She was silent: I did not know why. I loved her, but I could not understand what I was supposed to do about it. God: which did I love more—my music, or her? It did not matter: they deposited me near my tent. As I left the pickup, I put my fingers on her wrist. It was all so quick. I said thank you. And that was it. I finished my training and left with the division for Newport News, Virginia, and then sailed to Italy.

At 7 A.M., prodded by Captain Bucher and seeing others moving out through the trees, we got up, reluctantly, slowly, and followed. The company was spread out in a wide fan. We started down a slope; the hillside was slippery with dead leaves and the early morning dew. Orders were shouted left and right. It was all very confusing. I could hear shooting somewhere below us in the woods—and I was thinking . . . it's probably out of our range . . . don't worry about it boy. If it's going to get you it's going to get you no matter where you are. I've lost Holman! Where is he? . . . Oh, there he is. Better stay close. It's easier when there's someone to follow.

Lt. Sabin yelled back through the trees: "Hey! One of you throw a grenade in that dugout: we don't want to take any chances." Rebel tossed one in it. It exploded and dirt came flying out everywhere. No one bothered to look in. Then we stopped. "What the hell's the holdup!" "What! K Company?" "They haven't moved out yet?" "Goddamn it! What are they waiting on?" "We're dead ducks if the Krauts see us standing here!" "Hey! Where's that sniper firing from?" "Is he over there behind that ridge?" "Where'd Lt. Sabin go?" "I can't find Holman either!" "What do we do—run back up the hill, or dig in?" "Dig in—are you kidding?"

Then K Company appeared and we were off again, jumping and slipping around on the muddy slope of that hill. As we feared, the Germans spotted us and promptly began laying artillery fire on us.

No one knew quite what to do except that we all needed to find a safer place.

Sabin yelled back again: "Get over this ridge fast— and then you'd better dig in. We may stay here awhile." Utter confusion. Where should we go? But we had to move fast . . . it was no time to be choosy. I jumped out and landed under an overhanging bank. Two others landed with me: we all fell down together and squirmed so that we were lying side by side. GIs dropped all around us. None of us attempted to dig in: we expected to move out any moment. But the moments stretched into minutes and no orders came down. A shell screamed in just below us. No one was hit although shrapnel flew all over. Someone was yelling for a medic, but there were no medics around once again. The three of us raised up and looked down where the yelling was coming from. A GI had been hit in the face by shrapnel and was bleeding heavily. A sergeant with a sprained ankle offered to take him to the rear. I turned and watched them pass us: the sergeant was limping badly but had put his arm around the wounded soldier who was holding his shirt tight against his face. How in the hell, I thought, will they ever make it back alive? Then, unexplainably, I heard the wounded runner yelling for me—from yesterday—''Don't leave me to die, Bass!'' I saw him in the kitchen, in his white uniform, dishing out beans with his murky, unlovely face hanging ponderously over the steaming pot—and then I saw him again around the front lines, demoted from cook to runner, looking completely miserable and out of place outside the kitchen. Should I have stood up and risked my life to help him? His voice haunted me until another shell came in close. We were becoming impatient. Several times we tried to pass back word to Bucher and Sabin to find out what had gone wrong. Finally word came down to us that we were waiting for the 2nd Battalion to show up to support our right flank. In the meantime, the Germans had found our exact range and were now firing at us incessantly. Realizing how exposed we were, we had dug a little into the side of the bank and had piled the dirt around our feet. It was nerve wracking, the three of us lying side by side, each trying to gouge out the deepest hole, constantly in each other's way. Every time we heard the sound of incoming shells, we dropped and frantically squirmed into the soft earth. Woody Powers, a glib salesman from Chicago who laughed when a sniper's bullet grazed his skull on Mt. Belvedere, lay close behind me. Ruppert, small, gray-headed, with a reputation for throwing tantrums when he was upset, lay almost against my stomach. We agreed we were hungry and pulled out a K ration each and ate. I lay on my side, chewing, and studied the little whiskers on Ruppert's face. I could see each individual hair. He was old: each hair was almost white. Ruppert lay very calmly on his right side chewing his cheese and crackers. Some more shells came in.

The last one hit so close above us that it showered dirt all over us: clods of it rained on us like black hailstones. Woody, who had not been saying much, suddenly nudged me in the back.

"Here, Bassett—got something for you." I turned over and took a long sharp piece of shrapnel from his hand.

"Where'd you get this, Woody?"

"It fell right next to your back: in fact, it was touching your jacket."

"Throw it away, Woody. I don't want to look at it." In one glance I saw it was a whitish metal and that it had little fine, jagged edges. We started talking about taking off. The last shell had unnerved us.

"Come on, Gruenwald!" I yelled. Sergeant Gruenwald was dug in on top of the bank above us. He had almost lost it on Mt. Belvedere. He was at the base of the mountain, sitting by the trail while his own squad passed him up and the rest saw him there, apparently helpless and oblivious to the call of duty. I wrote him off as one of those GIs who just could not bear the strain of battle. But he had somehow survived that long night, and was now in the thick of it again. It was ironic that I appealed first to Gruenwald to run for safer ground. But he was the closest GI with a rank higher than mine. I needed a higher

26

authority to help me run. "Let's get out of here while we still can! We're sitting ducks!"

"You know the army, Bass—I can't—we shouldn't . . ."

Ruppert said he was going to take off and if the rest of us stayed there, well . . . we were crazy. But he waited. None of us wanted to be the first to go.

"What do you mean, Gruenwald?!" I yelled again. "The next shell could get us. Let's move and dig in again!"

Ruppert was the first to go. He grabbed his rifle and ran around and up the bank and on up the hill. That was all we needed. I ran, too, as did about five others, including Gruenwald. I could no longer reason it out—it was just time to run—anywhere, so long as it was far away from that place by the bank that smelled of burned earth and rotten leaves.

I looked down and saw Bucher and Sabin—both lying safe in their holes.

"Not here! Not here!" Bucher screamed, "Get over on the other side of the ridge! Gowan! Gowan!" And I went.

We climbed halfway up the hill before any more shells came in. Then two crashed in below us. Gruenwald and Sgt. Johnson were completely hidden from sight by the smoke. I was certain they had been hit. I looked again, and there they came through the smoke, unharmed.

I searched the side of the hill desperately for a spot without trees. But it was useless. Fuck it! I'd have to take a chance, that was all. Above me I saw where a shell had gouged out a big hole. I headed for it. I jumped in—it was much too wide and shallow—but I could dig—so long as I wished to live, I could dig. The earth was so loose and soft that it kept falling

27

into the hole: that was the only good thing; it was easy digging.

One of the GIs who ran with us had lost his shovel, and since I was alone, he came over and lay down beside the hole. I knew he wanted me to take him in—he just wouldn't say so. I ignored him at first. Tough shit, I thought. If he can't hang on to his shovel, that's his worry, not mine.

"Help me, Bass: I'm hit in the stomach! Don't leave me here to die!" The voice of the wounded runner from yesterday was crying for me again. I couldn't stand it—what if the new GI lying by the hole were hit?

I motioned to the sad face looking down at me. "Come on—come on down. Here—do you want to dig for awhile? We need to make this hole bigger." We knelt in the hole and shoveled out the dirt, packing it as best we could around the edge. Our new location was safer: shells kept coming, but they were not close.

Then I heard voices below us and got up to see who was approaching. Sgt. Stan Kuschick and Deb Jennings were coming up the hill. A few GIs were with them. Stan was mad because we had taken off: "What the fuck are you—what did you run for?"

"We had no orders to stay, and we were being hit."

"Where is your squad leader? Holman—where is Holman?"

"Don't know. There were no orders—we just all ran." Kuschick's face was a dark, stormy red and he snarled at us and said we were a sad lot of men. We waited. I had never seen him so upset. Stan was always good natured at Camp Swift. He always made a joke if the heat became unbearable on a long march and we threatened to drop out and fall in the shade by the road.

"Come on, you Sunday school mountaineers! Are you going to let this feeble Texas heat beat you? Let's show these flatlanders how a mountain troop can take it! We proved we could make it when it was twenty below zero—now let's show these big-mouthed Texans how we can take it when it's one hundred *above* zero!" With encouragement like this, a few of us never dropped out of any speed march, nor any long hike under the brutal Texas sun.

"Come on, Bassett. Yes, I said you! We're going up there on top of the hill to get a machine gun nest . . . the one nobody got yesterday!" The GI and I said nothing. Kuschick turned away and we followed him. The shellfire had not let up. The Kraut machine gun was shooting way above us. We picked our way up slowly. It was necessary to rest often. No one said anything: Kuschick knew when it was time to stop.

Near the top of the hill, we ran across my old buddy, John Breu, and Harpy Wheeler, who'd captured five German prisoners. They'd come out of a pillbox somewhere and surrendered. We stopped for a moment and asked if they needed help. They said no, so we kept moving. We were too large a group standing together. We moved quickly out of there, and somewhere near the top of the hill I became separated from Sgt. Kuschick and his little band of men, and from his mission to destroy the machine gun nest. I found myself running along the top of the hill. I realized at once that I had become a prime skyline target. But now I knew where I was going: I was going back to our positions we had left that morning. The offensive had stalled. I did not know why, and I did not care why. I was running good and free of obstacles along through the trees. I ran until a shell burst about fifty yards away from me. I saw a pillbox so I stopped and crouched down in front of it, and would have gone in except I saw it was jampacked full of GIs.

"Hey! You crazy fool!" they yelled from inside the pillbox. "Get off the hilltop! What are you trying to do—get us all killed?!" I was popular as a rattle-snake. I ran away and thought: what right do they have to yell at me like that? Lying snug and safe in there while I was outside dodging shrapnel and bullets? Had they been hidden there all day? Was Kuschick right? Were we all that day just a bunch of fucking cowards?

I ran down the reverse side of the hill and reached the holes safely. The whole reverse slope was covered with men in slit trenches. Here and there a few were empty so I jumped into one that looked good. It was just long enough—about three and a half feet deep with rocks laid carefully around the edges. Clothes and K rations belonging to the departed GI were lying around everywhere.

Sgt. Miller of the 1st Platoon came into sight below me. He looked old that afternoon. "Well," he said slowly, "they got Shipwreck Larson—right between the eyes . . . We'd told him all afternoon to stay down, but he wouldn't." I knew who he was. He was a quiet homely Dutchman who had volunteered for steady KP because, as he had told me once, "at least I'm doing something useful, which is better than killing, which is not." A dirty, thankless job he had asked for: cleaning out greasy pots with lukewarm muddy water that we'd already used on our messkits. It was a shame that he had to get it, when all he'd had to do was sit in his hole and keep his head down.

I had been without water most of the day: seven hours on the other side of the hill had made me very thirsty. There were plenty of water cans around, but they were mostly empty. The few containing water were being rapidly drained. I found a little water: enough for my canteen. The departed GI had left his mountain jacket filled with personal things: a wallet with photos of his family, a letter to a girl. I could not help myself, I had to read it:

April 15, 1945

Dearest Jennifer,

I have not heard from you in many weeks. I don't know why—maybe the mail was bombed or torpedoed along the way. So I will write to you again. I must tell you first that I miss you just terrible. Spring has come to this country and it makes me wish I could be there at home with you as the cherry and apple blossoms fill the orchard. Yes, I am homesick for the farm, and for you. I miss the times we swam in the lake on hot Sunday afternoons. Remember how we did it? I changed my clothes on one side of the old Hudson Terraplane, and you did the same on the other side. Then we ran to the shore and jumped in that cold blue water. We swam a little and then crawled up on the old rotten dock and lay down and shivered until the sun warmed us up again. And then we kissed each other. I loved you, Jennifer, then, and I love you so much now I can't tell you. But I'm waiting for the day when I'll return—for I *will* return. And we'll take the old car down to the lake and we'll swim and I'll put my arms around your beautiful body, and then—and then we'll drive to Ithaca and find a minister and we'll get married. What do you say to that? Is that alright? Please write and tell me so.

Forever Yours,
George

P.S. I want to tell you how

The unfinished letter lay on the edge of the trench with a fountain pen along side it.

"Hey! Over there!" I yelled to the nearest trench, "Do you know if this guy is coming back?"

"No, he went with the tanks. They ain't comin' back," was the answer. I found some crushed dry cereal wrapped in cellophane in his pockets. Ahh— this would be good. Mixed with water and sugar in my canteen cup . . . stirred well, would be quite a treat for my empty stomach. I didn't want to use his stuff, but if he wasn't coming back. . . .

I lay back in my new hole and drank some water and began to worry. I was worried about Sgt. Kuschick and the way he looked and acted. Maybe he was looking for me and when he found me in the hole, he would call me a coward to my face and I would have to leap up and follow him to the machine gun nest, where, in order to salvage my military record, I would have to wave Kuschick and the others down while I crept forward on my stomach to the bushes in front of the Kraut machine gun. Then, twenty yards from the pillbox, I would crawl with lightning speed to the box and insert a hand grenade with the pin pulled out through the opening. A muffled explosion would follow with plenty of black smoke pouring out of the opening. There would be silence then—no sign of life, and so I would withdraw and find Kuschick and collapse in his arms, an honest hero at last. But Kuschick did not come and I remembered that I was going to eat some cereal. I mixed the stuff up and ate it along with a fruit bar and some raisins from Fresno, California and some peanuts. It didn't make me or my stomach happy. I began to gag on the mess and threw most of it away. My cup sat in the dirt, sticky and gooey. There was no sand, so I pulled out some tissue paper and wiped it clean.

Above me, beside a CP dugout, some GIs were gathered around two German prisoners. One GI, who spoke German, was questioning them. They seemed very willing to answer his questions. I could hear some of the English translations now and then. They said the only reason they were fighting was because fanatic SS men held guns to their backs and forced them to fight. If our advance had not stopped this morning, they said, their troops could not have done a thing . . . easy victory would have been ours. I did not like their looks: they were both small, with flaxen hair and pasty white faces. They wore black steel helmets, green uniforms, and knee-high black boots. They were very happy to have been captured and be assured of decent treatment. As they started down the hill with their guard, the smaller one turned and said "Auf Wiedersehn." No one answered. We just watched them as they picked their way carefully down the hill.

It seemed to me, as I looked around the hillside covered with trenches, that half of all our men had stayed back there that morning when we had pushed off. I asked a few GIs around me if they'd known about it. "No," they assured me. "We had no instructions to move out . . . we were still asleep at seven," etc., etc.

"How was it out there?—pretty rough?" Some even asked if we'd taken the company objective: a big hill across the valley. The questions were maddening. Seeing them sitting around in their holes, taking it easy and eating was almost too much. I wanted to get it out of my system by yelling at them at the top of my voice that they were cowards—yellow bellies. But I didn't. I only sat and stared vacantly at them. What good was it to yell anyway? Looking at me, dirty and wild looking as I was, they'd only think I'd lost my mind or something. So I didn't show my feelings. Only inside was there that dull pang of anger and not knowing what to do. I didn't know who was right, or wasn't right, and I didn't know what to believe or what not to believe. I did know that it was all wrong— the whole thing. It was wrong because some men had died needlessly out there when they still could have been living—back with the others who breathed the fresh spring air on the reverse slope.

What the hell was that commotion up there? Somebody yelling? Here he comes. Getting dark now. . . . can't make out who it is. He came running towards us, shouting into each hole: "What are all you men doing back here? You can't all be in the reserve company! How the hell do you expect to win the war sitting back here?" He kept on going, demanding of GIs here and there what company they were from and giving them all hell.

Who the hell was he, anyway? Doesn't he realize it's too late for that kind of talk now? Wonder what excuse I would give him if he jumped on me, even though I'm waiting to move out again? Just a fool blabbing off his mouth I guess . . . To hell with him. He didn't come back. Somebody probably shut him up. It was nearly dark. Word came along the hill that the men out front were coming back and that everyone could stay put. I thanked the Almighty and considered how fortunate I was to have found an empty hole. A weight had been magically lifted from my shoulders.

"Hey! John T.—Hey! Is that you?" a voice suddenly called down to me. It was Holman, and in his voice were both anxiety and relief.

"Yeah, John, it's me alright. I see you made it too."

"You bet—glad to see you're still around." At such a moment, when two comrades find they have been spared, it is hard for the right words to come out. So there were no more words, but in my heart I was thankful that Holman had made it back.

Day was gone now, and night filled her place with darkness. I put on the mountain jacket and lay down, using my helmet liner for a pillow. Covering the center of the trench was an oblong slab of stone. When I lay down, I had to curl myself around it. I dropped off immediately into a fitful slumber. After lying so long in one unnatural position, it was necessary to move, and I did this the rest of the night. I must have changed over (head to foot) dozens of times. It grew colder and the stone grew even colder.

April 16, 1945

I AWOKE, LAME AND DRUGGED. A DENSE FOG OB-
scured everything. A good break. There would be no
artillery fire until it cleared. There was nothing to
do—yet. Holman must still be asleep. I began to
shiver. The fog was heavy. Everything was wet. I
sank back down in the trench and drifted off again. I
dreamed I was a child again, skiing down the long
slopes of the golf course above my home. I was skiing
alone in the dark when the demons of the night came
crying out of the dark woods around me and one
landed on my back like a gigantic bat and cackled
and talked and screamed into my ears. It told me I
was afraid of the night, and of him, my archenemy,
the Eternal Prince of the Night. I was terrified, of
course, and tried to shake it loose, but it clung there
and filled me with more fear than any nightmare
imaginable, until I skied through some walking skiers.
This encounter finally drove the demon off and I finished my ski run in tears, frightened, but impressed
with my courage in staying on my skis and not col-
lapsing in the snow and surrendering myself to the
demon. Then it was springtime, and I was walking
through a deep glen, alone. All the snow, and most
of the icicles, had melted. I could hear nothing but
the roar of the water as it gathered up melting snow

37

and ice along the way and poured over the waterfalls in huge brown cascades. I walked under a waterfall and stood back against the wall and shivered with the violent spray and trembled at the mighty force that roared out above me. And then I was sitting on a dock by the lake, a great cold inland body of water created by glaciers. The air was hot. I wore an old pair of shorts. Pretty Samantha ran down to the beach from her home and saw me. "Hi," she said in her cheerful voice. "Are you going for a swim?"

"In a minute," I said. "Right now I'm kind of tired."

"OK," she said. She stepped into a small shed at the water's edge, and in a moment reappeared wearing a brief, clinging bathing suit. She waved at me and ran out the full length of the dock and dove gracefully into the cold blue water. She surfaced and swam toward me. As she drew close, I saw one of her shoulder straps slip off her shoulder. I saw her chest, tanned brown, first, and then her breast, white and firm, rippling through the water. I had heard a few stories about Samantha. I had heard she often swam naked in the lake when the weather was hot and she thought no one was looking. She saw me watching her. She smiled and turned over on her back and swam away, her breast still exposed, and then disappeared around the edge of the dock.

I had had an erection when I walked into the home of my friend Peter in the morning and, in the hallway, we found her vacuuming the rug. I saw at once that his mother was wearing a very loose gown: it was not a bath robe; perhaps it was her night gown. In any event, as she pushed the vacuum cleaner along, the gown kept slipping off her shoulders. Her breasts were white and large and beautiful. I quickly grabbed Peter by his shoulders and stood directly behind him as I watched her, fascinated with her body and with the growing sensation in my penis.

A voice was calling me: calling me from above. Gradually I heard my name: "John T.—John T.—get up, get up, we're moving out in an hour. You hear me? Do you?"

Reluctantly I let the soft sweet dream go. There was no sex in a trench. Sex had to happen where there was a soft bed, or a soft field in summer—but never could there be sex in a trench. I awoke again.

"OK—OK, Holman, I'm awake. What? In an hour? OK, OK, I'll be ready."

I ate most of a full K ration and decided not to take the mountain jacket. I folded up the departed GI's letter and put it in a pocket of his jacket with the fountain pen and laid it at one end of the trench.

We heard now that it was pointless to "capture" any more hills. It was fairly evident that the Germans were retreating. We were going down to the roads that led north and try to overtake them before they gathered somewhere and fought little battles against us.

We climbed out of our holes and filed down to a dirt road below. The fog prevented any sniper fire. Down on the road we stopped again. "Hey! Up there! Pass it up—they stopped again!" The GIs coming down the steep embankment halted in place.

"What's up now for Christ's sake?"

"I don't know. They just stopped—no word." There were red Kraut wire lines strewn around, mostly all cut, and a few helmets, covered with dust. The longer we waited, the more GIs there were who lay down in the ditches. It was all a matter of timing. A nap in the ditch was worth it if it could stretch into fifteen minutes. Otherwise, no because it took too much effort to get up again.

I was restless. Was it possible for the Krauts to direct any artillery fire on that road? I maintained a constant vigil. As long as I was on the line, there was danger. Some of our heavy mortars located nearby were firing at regular intervals. The loud sharp reports made us jump.

Then we got some good news. Two I Company jeeps came bumping along the road and stopped when they saw us. Pat, our supply sergeant, and his assistant, and the driver, Milhawlin, had faces coated thick with yellow-white dust. They looked like grotesque tragedians from another century. Pat told us that the Brazilians were coming up to relieve us that night. Everyone became a little excited. Smiles broke out. They believed Pat. In the other jeep was a big box full of doughnuts. The driver passed them out. He was careful—he was very watchful to see that no one got more than one. We sat around a little longer and then the word came back to saddle up: the line was moving again.

"Crossroads ahead!" came the warning. "Keep ten yards." There were crushed bricks and glass lying all over, and the ruins of two houses. Italian and German road signs pointed towards the north. A little farther and we saw two American heavy tanks concealed behind some houses.

"What the hell stinks?"

"Something's dead alright."

"Hey! Watch out or you'll step on it!" There was a rotting carcass of a cow in the path. The odor was suffocating. I noticed it was nearly all dried up. A few more steps and the odor was gone. Small hills to our immediate right flank protected us from observation by the Krauts, who we figured were across the valley somewhere. After an hour, we stopped behind a line of woods. In their shade many slit trenches had already been dug, and they were fairly deep. They had been recently vacated. K ration boxes and trash lay all over, together with some Kraut helmets and clothing. We all found holes and got settled. Sabin was busy selecting the holes that would be used for guard duty. A GI that I simply called the straw-haired boy and I found a good one. We only had to widen it a little. The GIs before us had left some cardboard for the bottom. There was the usual heated argument over who stood guard and when. I wanted an early shift so I could sleep most of the night. The straw-haired boy and I were on from ten to midnight the first night. It was very dark, and a cool breeze was fingering my neck when one of the guards woke me (while the other guard nervously awaited his return).

"Hey, Bassett, Hey! . . . Wake up!" he whispered loudly. "Time to go on!" I woke up easily enough and whispered back:

"OK, I'm awake." The black crouched form leaning over my hole disappeared.

I lay there a minute longer looking at the stars twinkling faintly far overhead. I knew I could rely on them. I did not know their names—but that was not important. I knew by the stars that the earth was turning, and if the night seemed endless, I could look at the stars and watch it slowly slip away.

I nudged my partner and he awoke. First, I threw off the raincoat that had covered us both from our waists down, then I pulled on my boots. Last, the steel helmet: my pillow, my wash basin, and also my insurance against insanity. I was aware of the deep stillness of the night as my buddy and I groped un-

41

certainly around the holes for the path that led to the outpost. It pounded in my ears, making me deaf to all the little noises I was straining so hard to hear. I was tight all over: fear was making me clumsy. I still couldn't see anything, so I had to feel my way. The dead leaves rustling under my feet are a sure give-away, I thought.

"Halt!" the command was given in a low urgent voice. "Give the password."

"Lillian." I gave the first word. I could see them now, they were standing together in their shallow hole, nearly invisible.

"Woodrow." They answered with the last word, and the short, necessary formality was over.

"Boy, are we glad to see you guys," one said as we crouched down by the hole. "This has been a long two hours."

"Yeah? Anything happen tonight? Any 88s come in?"

"No, it's been quiet as a church out here. I thought I saw a light out to the left front once; maybe where we saw those houses with the Red Cross markings on them. That's all."

"Yeah—OK—where's your watch? OK, I got it—we'll take over now—yeah, take it easy going back and keep to the right; you'll find the path easier."

I lay two grenades on the edge of the trench within easy reach, the rifle too. The helmet stayed on: I felt better with that weight on my head. There was nothing else to do but lean back and watch and listen and wait. Every half hour I had to report in on the telephone to the sergeant at the company CP that everything was OK. I could hear the others calling in too; their voices were reassuring. During the long intervals we were still. We were afraid to move or make any kind of noise for fear we'd miss a sound out there. It was easy to imagine that a German patrol was creeping up on our hole and that a well thrown grenade would end it all for my buddy and me. I stayed awake—very much awake.

A sudden swaying of a branch in the night wind caused me to momentarily freeze. An icy shiver ran through my body, and though I knew at once that it was nothing, a prickly sensation kept running up and down the back of my neck. It was something I always felt when there was danger. I wondered too what I would do if a German rushed me. My eyes searched the outlines of the gray and black shadows to my front, then to the sides, and always to the rear.

Perhaps another outpost thought they saw something out front and reported it. Anyway, suddenly some of our artillery came whistling over the hill and burst in rapid succession about three hundred yards below our position. The shells fell way short, and some shrapnel slithered into the ground near our hole.

Someone was whistling in the phone and calling "Baker two" (our post number). The whistle was to get our attention. I answered it. Sgt. Penny's voice from CP came over the wire:

"Oh, say Bassett, were those coming in or going out?"

"They were definitely ours, Penny. They whistled directly over our position."

"Uh—OK, Bassett, just checking; didn't know for sure. They sounded a little close. How'd they look to you?"

"They landed down in the valley where those houses are. I guess somebody saw a light down there."

"Yeah, umm . . . well, OK Bassett." Apparently

he was satisfied. And no more shells flew over our heads.

"Looks like we aren't being relieved tonight," I said to my companion.

"Nope, I guess not; maybe they'll come tomorrow." The rest of the time passed quietly.

"I'll go wake up Rebel and Ruppert now. It's about ten 'til twelve," my companion said, "OK?"

"Do you know where they sleep for sure?"

"Yeah, just left of our hole."

"OK, go ahead." He collected his equipment and took off in a hurry. After a few anxious moments they appeared. I halted them and they were identified.

"How's things out here, boy?" asked Rebel as he unslung his rifle.

"Pretty good, Rebel, she's all quiet tonight." I kind of liked Rebel, but I didn't know why. I first noticed him in the mess hall at Camp Swift with his good buddy, Schuck. My teeth were bothering me so I was late in finishing the evening meal. Rebel and Schuck were eating fried chicken across the table and enjoying the meal immensely. They talked as they ate, but I saw that they ate with dedication: they cleaned the wings, the legs, the thighs, the backs of the meat, the fat, the skin, and they gnawed on the bones voraciously. Schuck was a great big shapeless hunk of young man. He was from the deep south, as was Rebel. I did not get to know Schuck. After Mt. Belvedere was taken, I wandered across a field and saw a fire blowing up and down in front of a GI sitting in the field. It looked peculiar so I went over to the GI to see what he was doing. There was Rebel, sitting, with his equipment close by. He was holding a lighted blow torch under a large metal can.

I came up to Rebel and said: "What in the hell are you doing?"

"Why, Bass—can't you see? I'm makin' some french fries."

"French fries?!" I exclaimed, "I don't believe you!"

"Look, man, look," he said. I dropped down on my knees and saw he told the truth. He had the can sitting on a flat stone. It was full of potato slices and they were being fried in grease. The blow torch was lit and he played a blue flame over the can. I saw that the grease was bubbling. I dropped down in the dirt beside Rebel.

"Where—where did you find this torch?" I asked.

"Had it all along, in my pack—figured a day would come when I could use it. There—that should be good enough. Want to try my cooking, Bass?"

"Why, yes, Rebel, but I can't believe it—real french fries?"

"Here, try one." He took a fork and pulled a brown sizzling slice of potato out of the can. I took it gingerly between my fingers and took a small nibble. It was hot. I waved it to and fro and then took a bigger bite. Rebel nodded approvingly. I wolfed it down. Rebel took the rest of the slices out of the can.

"Here, Bass, have some more."

I lay down by the rock and ate several slices. "Where'd you get this grease?" I asked.

"From the kitchen: they knew I had a blow torch."

"But, the potatoes? Where'd you get them?"

"Right here in this field."

"You knew there were potatoes in this field?"

"I grew up on a farm in Alabama: we grew potatoes, cotton and corn. I dug up potatoes from the time I was eight years old. I reckon I know a field has potatoes the minute I step in it. Yeah, now ain't that good, Bass? I reckon we're the only ones in this division eatin' french fries right now—heah, have some more." Southern hospitality at its best, I thought. Rebel kind of lay back against his pack and wielded the blow torch like a true chef. He was slight of build, with a pale narrow face, and he was growing a long goatee. He lay back and stroked his goatee with his left hand while he cooked potatoes with his right hand. There was a philosophical air about him and what he was doing.

"You see, Bass, this is how we live in the south. The land provides it all if you treat the land right. My grandpappy had a hundred acres. He had a grist mill. He raised cotton. He had some cattle, hogs, and chickens. He had enough to feed us and to sell too. There, those taters are done—take some out and eat. Bass, we're in the midst of a terrible conflict. I pray every night that it will turn out alright for us." He lay back on his pack and looked gravely at the can full of bubbling potatoes.

"Well, Rebel," I said, pushing myself up reluctantly from the soft earth, "I got to thank you for this treat. These french fries are the greatest food I've ever eaten in my life."

Rebel leaned forward and shut off the flame on the torch.

"I'm glad you came over to see me, Bass. Maybe we'll do this again someday."

"Yeah—yeah, it was great, Rebel; got to get back to our position up on the hill. See you later." I left Rebel with a sad feeling in my heart.

Now Ruppert and Rebel eased themselves into the hole.

"Well," I said, "here's the watch: it's all yours." And I went back to my hole with the straw-haired boy.

April 17, 1945

THE NEXT MORNING WE LAY AROUND IN THE SUN
and relaxed. Degutis came down wearing his Limey
cap and his usual broad smile. He had some Kraut
snapshots and a cane. We all looked at them. The
man in the photos was middle-aged. He looked genial
enough, and seemed to be enjoying an outing with
his family.

"Hey, Degutis," someone asked, "where'd you get
this stuff?"

"Off one of those dead Krauts over there in the
field." I liked Degutis. He was charming, always
smiling, but he always sought out the German dead
and robbed them. He was never reprimanded for this.
No one seemed to care. It was war, and that ac-
counted for it.

I went on guard again at noon. During the day only
one GI now stood guard at the outpost. I had a different hole too. It was closer to the CP, but it was
shallow; not really a hole at all. It could have been a
very pleasant two hour stretch. I was comfortable
enough lying back in the shallow trench, and the day
was warm and sunny. A cupful of cereal and water
and some candy-coated peanuts were by my side,
waiting to be eaten. I was reading a week-old issue
of Stars and Stripes and not worrying much because

the Krauts seemed to have called it quits for a while. But there was something on my mind, and it bothered me. Just before I got into the trench, I had made an unpleasant discovery. Coming out here last night, I must have passed close to it. I was hard; I was tough now, but still a shiver went through me. It was only another GI corpse. But why—at this time—did I have to see it? Just when I was about to relax for two hours? I knew it was thawing in the warm sun . . . at night it would grow stiff again. I tried to concentrate on the paper, but my interest somehow was gone. The branches swaying gently in the breeze attracted my eye and when I thought of the cereal, I wasn't hungry at all. Anyway, there were big black flies buzzing all over and some lit on the cup.

Later in the afternoon four Krauts, guarded by a single GI, came up a trail carrying a stretcher. They were coming to take back the dead, theirs and ours. They would find many of their own countrymen. I had carried American and German corpses back from the front during the winter just past. It wasn't so bad handling corpses in cold weather. They were frozen and if they fell off the litter, I didn't get all messy . . . and there was no smell. Now that the days were warm, I prayed I would not be put on that detail again.

The rumors were strong that we were going to be relieved that night by the Brazilians. We really believed it when two Brazilian officers came up at sunset to look over the area. One of the officers was very distinguished looking: dark and slim and mustached. He made Sabin look like a rookie.

Everything remained calm and peaceful until dusk. We were all eating and sitting around when the quiet was suddenly and rudely interrupted by two shells that exploded in the woods fairly close to our camp.

It was peculiar—no one heard them come in. Just two explosions and shrapnel zipping close overhead. We all jumped for our holes like big two-legged frogs. There was a period of silence. I could not hear a sound. Everyone was waiting and wondering if there would be more. I never actually knew what silence was until then, when my buddy and I were lying in that hole, hugging the ground and holding our breath so we could hear better. Outside there was only the fading light and silence. The world we had known and had lived in seemed to have stopped, and all the living things in it vanished—all but the two of us— who lay waiting in the eternity of silence. Then I heard a voice and the spell was broken. "Hey Blackie! Did you happen to see where they hit?"

"Nuh uh, Penny." Blackie shook his head. "I never heard 'em until they hit." It became dark and we turned in without further incident. The Brazilians wouldn't come until the wee hours in the morning, we were told. Sleep came quickly. Night lay heavily in the valleys and ravines and all the smaller holes and depressions of the earth. It was a time of mercy. Stilled figures, cold and grisly on the face of the earth, were given another relief from the harsh revealing light of day, and from the curious stares of the living. Yes, for the dead it was merciful. But for the living, the hellish ordeal went on. Night for us was a time of patrols, of unseen movements in the grass, of deadly suspense. For us night was unfathomable . . . perhaps that was truest of all.

Someone pushed my foot and I woke up. "Get your stuff together; the Brazilians are here."

There was confusion: where were they anyway? They were certainly not here . . . What? Oh . . . They're coming eh?, and should be here in a few minutes? . . . Good deal!! I had visions of Montecatini again; that neat little medieval resort town, and comfortable cots. It would be wonderful to get three hot meals a day. And there would be PX rations, candy, cookies and peanuts. I could sleep and not be afraid for a few days. We were ready to go but they still hadn't come. We waited and watched the trail anxiously for any signs of them. At last we saw them coming. They came up to us and began babbling to each other. They sounded cheerful, even indifferent, in their attitude towards the fighting, or so it seemed.

After a lengthy discussion with their leader, Sabin finally got away and we started down the hill. On the road below we halted and sat down in place. There was something fishy in the air. It was funny how I could sense it: I just had a feeling that something was going wrong. We moved across the road down to our approximate position of two days ago.

"Say," someone whispered, "I heard we aren't going back tonight. I'll bet that's what happens too."

It occurred to me all at once that was what I'd felt would happen. The next thing I knew another line was going past us on the other side of the road, heading north. The rumor was true. I could forget the rest: we were going north too. I stood up and watched the other column. I could see for myself the mystery and anxiety, the weariness and comedy and monotony that was the line. Dim figures in the gray-black gloom. The tall ones with their easy stride, the short ones who half ran, half trotted to keep up. Figures that bounced along confidently, their messkits rattling faintly, and figures that moved methodically, determinedly. I saw the tired, the lagging, and I wondered if they'd last. Half-heard mutterings, a curse here and there . . . a laugh . . . they drifted past us and were gone.

The mystery was with us too, for a reason that no one understood; we did not complain, there was no bitching. The other column had been exciting to watch. They were headed for unknown adventure— could I call it that?—and plenty of danger and the promise of death lurked on up the trail ahead. The word came for us to move out. We stood up silently and our feet found the road and we did not walk, we moved, a body of men geared for battle in the night; a sinister force, prepared to kill whatever stood in our way and threatened us. We thought the Krauts were evil; but we were evil too. I was prepared to kill a man, or men for a crime or crimes he or they may not have committed. Should it be right for me to kill a middle-aged Kraut who loved his family and believed in God, not in Hitler, but who was drafted by the Third Reich to serve his country? I could not stop to think it out: the line dictated that I follow it obediently, and since I was a good soldier, I did so.

For no apparent reason, the line began to accelerate. Soon I was running to keep up with the GI in front of me. When he slowed, I would bump into him and apologize for it. Then we were running again to the tune of our gasping breath and the dull clumping sound that our boots made on the road. Again the line slowed down. In a few minutes I began to shiver in my own sweat . . . my shirt clung to my back, cold and clammy. In the top of my head there seemed to be a peculiar lightness. My eyes smarted from their intense concentration, and little red and white specks jumped around in the dark in front of me. The change was swift: if it was too swift . . . well, the road was always ready. It had room to receive the weary, the wounded, the dead.

Then suddenly, the road ended in a field. A GI led Sabin to a small mountain of packs. We picked up a pack each. Two blankets had been stuffed into each pack. In the morning the packs were to be returned to their owners. It was very late: Sabin led us to the edge of the field where there was a bank with trees above it. We were not ordered to dig in; just spread out along the bank so that we had protection on one side. I found a fairly comfortable place next to the bank and crawled under my blankets. An enormous tree towered over me above the bank. Its limbs flung out far and wide. I looked up at it and was a little afraid. What if a shell were to hit it: a tree burst could be fatal . . . how could a shell miss those outstretched branches . . . I was so exhausted the fear slowly seeped out of my mind, and I slept. But in my sleep I had a dream that I wandered in a strange forest, and that the very trees became monsters that turned their branches into arms and hands and they reached out to grab me. But before I was snatched up, I saw a girl coming to my rescue, and with her was a radiant witch waving a wand at the monster trees. I recognized Dorothy at once from the Wizard of Oz. She and the wonderful witch saved me. I looked into Dorothy's eyes and knew I loved her very much. I reached out to kiss her, but the witch enveloped her in her golden gown, and they flew off. Kansas, I must go to Kansas. I struggled furiously and found I had thrown off my blankets. I sat up on the lumpy ground and looked around me. It was only a dream. I was in a field in Italy. Kansas was very far away.

April 18, 1945

THE KITCHEN WAS SET UP IN THE FIELD AND WE HAD some hot chow that morning. The dehydrated eggs were OK. The bread and jam was much better, so I had more. Then I returned the pack to the pile, and looked for mine.

It took me quite a while to find it: I wasn't feeling well, and stumbled and fell among the mountain of packs and finally located it. Soon afterward, Holman handed out some new C rations to his squad. Each man got three heavy units and three light ones. The three heavies were usually spaghetti and meat balls; beef and noodles; meat, beans, and vegetable stew. The three light units were breakfast, dinner, and supper cans. The breakfast had a package of crunched cereal, another of powdered cocoa, and one of candied peanuts and raisins. The dinner had six soda crackers, orange drink powder and a few hard candies. The supper had six crackers, about five caramels and lemonade or orange drink powder. Sometimes I drew more than one of each. In the case of the heavy units I tried to trade the duplicates off with someone else, but I could never get rid of beef and noodles or the meat and vegetables. Eaten cold, these two were a sticky clammy mess of unseasoned, plain, tinny-tasting guck.

The rest of the morning went by rapidly. The sun was too hot to allow us much rest. I used to sunbathe back in basic training in Florida. No matter how tough the march, when the line stopped and there was a break, Breu, my buddy, and I threw ourselves on the ground, put our heads on our steel helmets and took the sun like two demented tourists. Then, if we were near a shady forest pool, we would jump in the dark water fully clothed, rifle and all, and emerge grinning, looking foolish, inviting criticism from our lieutenant, but feeling a new sense of independence that was not far removed from rebellion. Now, however, it was different; there was no stream. While it was too hot now, when night fell, the air would be too cold. So I lay and squirmed and sat up and endured the heat.

Holman was called to a meeting with Captain Bucher, along with the other squad leaders. In a half an hour he was back, and we gathered around him to find out what the story was. General Hays had decided to abandon the attempt on a nearby objective. Instead, we would now head for the Po Valley as fast as we could, to try and bottle up the Krauts in the Brenner Pass, and prevent them from escaping Northern Italy. Well, we saw that a rat race was in the offing: the faster we could march, the farther we could go in a day's time, and the better General Hays would like it. Of course, they would ride along side us in their jeeps and give us encouragement and wave the flag and a few bottles of Italian vino at us and escape in clouds of dust as we looked after them, hot and dry, and we would curse them softly because we bore the burden of the battle. We ate all the dust and saw no champagne at the end of the day's march.

Holman concluded by saying that we'd carry light

packs: bare essentials. The rest we would put in our shelter halves and they would be carried in trucks until we could use them again. We would be ready to move out at one o'clock that afternoon. The morning was gone now, and it wouldn't be long until we moved out again. Some of the GIs opened another can of C rations and ate again. I opened a light unit and ate some candy and fixed a cup of lemon drink. Holman went around and checked to see if everyone was ready. I had two blankets, a raincoat, my writing kit, two pairs of socks, and the C rations.

At one we formed up and waited for the order to move out. There wasn't much talking. We were waiting for them to move out up ahead, and we were wondering what we'd see when we went over the bank at the edge of the field.

I looked up and the line was leaving the field. "Let's go! . . . come on, Carafa! We're waiting on you!" Bucher yelled. Sergeant Carafa, technical sergeant of the Second Platoon, smiled serenely and waved.

"I'll be right up, Captain, I'll be right up!" I smiled too. I knew a lot about Carafa. He was like Sabin: he was a born hero, but unlike Sabin, he had the air of a fine actor, and he was reckless. I admired Sabin, but I loved Carafa.

Out of the field we went. Things were pretty well banged up as we passed some abandoned Kraut dugouts. Empty cognac and champagne bottles and clothes and equipment littered the place. There was blood on some of the clothing. The dugouts were artfully placed and concealed. We looked at them curiously as we passed. We jumped down on a dirt road that followed the side of the mountain. As far as I could see the road wound in and out of the hills that

stretched northward. To the right, the mountain gradually fell away and I could see way off in a distant
valley a river that shimmered and sparkled in the sun.

The road was several inches thick with yellow pow-
dery dust. It wasn't long before I was covered with
it. On the backs of my hands and wrists, where I
sweat constantly, and on my eyelashes it clung. The
sun beat on my helmet furiously and kept my eyes
squinted and half-closed. Occasionally we passed
small bivouac areas where several large tents were set
up. They were mostly truck outfits or artillery battal-
ions. There were white markers along the road warning pedestrians not to venture off the sides too far:
there were still areas not cleared of mines.

Goddamn but it was hot! I had to watch my water.
It wouldn't pay in the long run to drink too much,
even though my lips and throat were bone dry. As
long as I continued to sweat I was alright because I
still had water and salt enough in my system to keep
me on my feet. If I stopped sweating on the march
then it was time to take a swig or two. We hiked
steadily for an hour and then took a break . . . another hour's march, and another break.

Back, way back on the road, a column of vehicles
was raising clouds of dust. They were coming our
way. We sat in the sun and watched them come. Due
to a holdup in the line somewhere we were still sitting
there when the column caught up with us. Medium
tanks were at the head of it. They rumbled by us with
their exhausts blowing the dust in our faces. The road
was very narrow and the long line of tanks, half-
tracks and trucks passed close to us. The roar of their
engines was deafening.

Once in a while we'd stick our feet out in the road
and pretend we were going to let them be run over.

It was an old joke with us; a squashed toe or foot was an easy way to get out of the front lines. Sometimes the tank drivers grinned at the crude joke to let us know they understood. We would always pull our feet back just in time.

"Let's go Third Squad. On your feet!" Holman yelled. The break was over. More hiking. The tanks and trucks came to a stop and we started passing them.

"Crest, change off on that BAR for awhile," Holman advised. Crest never asked anyone else to help him carry it. Recently he had appropriated a big engineer's shovel. He'd tied a rope to it and carried it slung over his shoulder wherever he moved. When he was through digging with it there were always eleven others waiting. I carried the BAR for a while. It weighed approximately twenty-one pounds.

I could tell as I passed the line of vehicles that my buddies and I were respected by the men who drove them. There were no encouraging remarks—or words or praise. It was something I felt in the silence. I had the feeling that I looked rugged and capable walking along with the BAR resting partially on my pack and right shoulder, while I steadied it with my hand.

There was a fork in the road ahead: one road went straight on, the other turned up a hill. The line of men was going up the hill. I knew it had been too good to be true: we'd be breaking our backs again in a minute. As soon as I hit the upgrade I leaned over a little. It was easier on my back and I could breathe better. The BAR was making me sweat. As usual, the line was moving twice as fast now that we were climbing a hill. We stopped for a minute. I was really getting tired: I'd carried that damn BAR long enough. "Here Fuller: you take it next—OK?"

"Alright, Bass—Fronk: I'll give it to you next, boy: this is a son of a bitch to carry—you know it?" He stood there with a resigned look on his face. Fuller was too old. He was thirty-seven. He had five kids at home. He was no hiker, no sportsman, no hunter after deer or ducks, or mourning dove. Fuller was a quiet, gentle sort who lived for his family. War was monstrous to him. It could have destroyed him, but he went through each day operating on faith. He simply believed that God would not separate him from his wife and children.

We went over the hill. It was a long afternoon. There were more and more tents and motor pools along the way—a few POW stockades here and there. Apparently the front lines were still far ahead. But then, motor pools and the rest were never within heavy artillery range of the front lines.

The road was in front of me—always in front of me. It was like a magnet; I looked at the budding trees, at the blue sky and the hills, and then my eyes came back irresistibly to the road, the same dusty road that had no end. I followed it and it said things to me. Sometimes they were frightening things, like the chant that rose mysteriously that day through the sound of the scuffing feet, marching ceaselessly, insistently, in a loose rhythmic step. Over and over I half thought, half heard the words that formed and spoke to me. You're a fool, a fool, a fool. They didn't accuse or reproach me: they seemed only to be sighing.

It was the low weary voice of the road, a mournful voice saddened through the centuries by the sight of countless thousands of young men who had trod this road to their deaths. You are young and you are a fool, it said, for this road will but lead you to your death. "You are a fool, a fool, a fool," it sighed. I heard and perhaps half comprehended, but I was young and the voice of the road was very old. For the young men who in ages past had marched on the road, and who marched again that day, never heeded it, nor seemed to care. We marched on and heard nothing but the sound of our own feet.

Ahead, another hill was alive with the long, slow crawling line of tanks, trucks and ambulances. It was a hot short hike up that hill. Them we were on top and going through a narrow defile. Then we were out and looking down and out at the green hills falling away, away until they became purple and merged into the horizon. A valley spread itself below us and it too descended gradually to the north. We knew now that the Appenines were behind us and we felt as though we were getting some place at last. It would be easier now: there were no more mountains to climb.

The line stopped again so we sat down on the edge of the road, our feet dangling over the side, and gazed at the new country. There was something exciting in the air. We knew the Po Valley lay just ahead. A veritable paradise, it supplied Italy with abundant crops and dairy products. It was the dream of every GI that if we made it to the Po, there he would find his just and deserving reward—(would it not consist mainly of milk and wine?). We'd heard enough about it and why the Germans were reluctant to leave, and now we wanted to see all those things ourselves.

The column of vehicles was barely missing us: the road was too narrow. Woody Powers yelled at Crest just in time to prevent a heavy tank with a plow on its front from hitting him in the back. It was a wicked looking plow: they were used to clear out roadblocks. We moved again. Way off to the left beyond the valley was another range of hills. The Germans probably still held them. I hoped they couldn't see us. Out straight ahead, I could see the column going along the road, kicking up individual clouds of dust. A tank was lying on its side just off the road. I wondered what had happened.

The road went down and curved through a grove of tall trees. God! The whole area was completely torn up with shell holes! My heart started jumping and I felt sweat break out on my forehead and hands. The line stopped again, under the tall spreading trees. "Keep ten yards!" The order was passed down the line. Behind us was the hill covered with trees and shell holes. In front of us, across the road, there was a small creek. Jack Mathews crossed over first to fill up his canteen. Others followed. I sat down beside the trunk of a big tree. The bigness of it made me feel better. But everyone was jittery: it was too quiet. There was a corpse lying on the side of the road: it was mostly all dust. It had been there awhile. No one sat near it.

Then some shells whistled in behind us. I saw the clouds of black smoke swirling up through the trees in the bright sunlight. The trucks and ambulances moved into high gear: they came roaring down around the bend and past us and scrammed out of there. The Germans had spotted the column and now the 88s came in fast after the first few. But, surprisingly, their aim was very poor. The shells hit the hills above us, too far away to do us any harm. The line started moving again—in a hurry. Ahead we saw the rubble of a small village. An MP stood there in the open directing traffic, doing his best to keep it moving. The shells were still coming over and hitting well above the road. The road went up a hill. Halfway up the hill the line stopped and we stooped down beside a protective large hedge. There were tanks going by . . . and then they stopped. Those bastards, I muttered. They'll draw more artillery fire on us. We began yelling at the tanks. We cursed them for stopping by us. They started rolling again, roaring mightily, and disappeared in their own dust over a hill.

The line moved, and we were glad to be off again. The pace began to quicken. We were in a hell of a hurry. The lush green fields were now close to us. The Germans stopped shelling us. Would there be a harvest that fall? Or would all the crops go to seed? The sun was sinking now, but it was still hot and we were going along fast and steady. My water was almost gone. During one short halt, a jeep stopped fifty yards behind me, and the driver opened up a water can for the men nearest him. I was lying on my back in the middle of the road. I wasn't in the mood to run back, even for a swallow. When the can was empty, the driver came by us saying he'd just drained his last can. I guess he knew how it was to be tired and dry.

Holman asked a lieutenant in a jeep if he knew where the 87th Regiment was. The lieutenant said the 87th was moving so fast all contact had been lost, and even the jeeps were finding it hard to get C rations up to them. Well, they were running: the Germans must really be hightailing it for the Brenner Pass.

Then I was up again and hoofing it up the road. The long ascent came to an end on an open grassy hill. All around there were fields of grass. In the west the sun was hovering over the hills. General Hays passed us there. He was going back. He was standing up and barking at the men to clear the way for his jeep. We passed a field hospital set up in a field on our left. They were all brown canvas tents lined up in neat rows, with the large red cross markings on the tops and sides.

The line turned off the road down a slope into a creek bed. The second platoon began digging in at once on the far side and we faced them from the near side. It was all alfalfa, it came up to our ankles. There was some hay scattered around below us. I ran down and scooped up an armful of it for our hole. Luca Luhaink and I were going to sleep together. Orders were that we must dig down to a depth of two feet— before dark. A faint drone of an airplane hummed persistently in my ears. I heard it but thought nothing of it because my mind was occupied with the digging. Then, like a hovering hawk that suddenly sees its prey, it went into a power dive. We all looked up as it pulled out with a sudden loud roar. A shuddering C-r-rump! Br-r-rump! followed as two bombs shook the earth. The word went around to keep all matches out. There was some arrangement about standing guard, but I wasn't worried about it. My feet were sore and my shoulders and back were stiff. I concentrated on my digging the hole. The ground was hard. The dirt came out in big chunks. I'd dig half heartedly for a couple of minutes and then lean back dejectedly on my ankles and look around and just sit. Then I'd come to, and realize that the light above the hills was becoming more pale and I'd fall to a fury of shoveling. It was just dark when we finished leveling off the hole, only a foot deep. The straw went in and we were ready to sleep. Lt. Sabin came through and told us we were getting up at five A.M. to continue the rat race. They couldn't find me so I slept through my guard duty, the whole hour of it. I didn't sleep well: the hole was too narrow and where my head was supposed to rest, the hole was too deep. I turned from one side to the other all night long. Each time I turned I looked at Luca sleeping sound as a baby all zipped up to his chin in his sleeping bag.

I fell asleep at last, muttering obscenities to myself, and drifted in my dream back to the little village of Prunetta where we had first been billeted. Someone said, "Come on, Bass: someone's playing the accordion in that house down the street." I ran after him and entered a cold room crowded with villagers. A man sat on a bare wooden table at one end of the room. He played melodies that were simple. The throng laughed and clapped and sang. I felt a growing pressure against my thigh. I saw that a girl in front of me was pressed hard against me so I could not move. She was my age; her hair was dullish blonde and poorly combed. I could not see much of her face, but it was the unrelenting pressure against my thigh that aroused me at last. Why did I not put my arm around her—why did I not try to whisper something to her? I could not speak Italian. But did that really matter? Was she not aware of her union with me? She did not look around, nor wiggle, nor move. I should have moved her somehow, but I could not. The accordion player quit playing, and the moment was lost—gone forever. The crowd of villagers left the room and the pressure was gone from my thigh. I looked then for her, but she, too, was gone. Back in my cold bed in a villager's home, I looked out the window. Then, slowly, it dawned on me: she was saying something to me. That hard, steady pressure was a message. She could not look at me, nor talk. But her body, her warm leg, told me that I was a man, and that she was a woman.

April 19, 1945

I OPENED MY EYES. HOLMAN WAS PUSHING ME AND saying: "What about Prunetta, John T.? What did you say about Prunetta?"

"Nothing," I said morosely. I was awake.

"Come on—come on, let's go, get up and eat. We're moving out soon. Let's go!"

There was salt in my eyes: who had put it there? And the lead weights on my eyeballs? There was pain throbbing behind them. I sat up and looked around. Dew was on my blankets and all over the slope. The sun wasn't up yet. I rose slowly and stood on my blankets while I reached for my combat boots. They almost would not go on, and when I took a few steps I wondered how many more steps I could take before my flesh swelled up and burst the leather. My rifle that had rested on my steel helmet all night was saturated with dew, and the helmet, too, glistened wetly. It was unbelievable the slope was that wet. My feet were soaked in no time. But it was also cool and fresh: was it not an ideal morning? The cool air made my eyes smart and caused me to shiver a little. I packed my gear and opened a can of dehydrated ham and eggs, and some crackers and orange drink. The crackers and drink went well together, but the ham and eggs were cold: they didn't go down right. I was still hungry, but I didn't want to gag anymore, so I threw the can away as far as I could. There was no waiting around that morning: the company formed up and we moved out just before sunrise.

Up on the road again, and on down the road. There were a few houses around, most of them deserted and ugly-looking-forbidding. Captain Bucher was walking slowly. The rest of us were like drugged patients who had gotten out of bed and were walking in a dream. Was there a war on this morning? The hand that was closed around my rifle sling was limp. It clung to the sling only from force of habit. The helmet pushed my head over a little so that I looked at my feet rising and falling—swinging along. I was dead tired and lame all over . . . I hurt. I wanted to lie down, nothing more. I felt there was only one worthwhile thing left in my dirty miserable life, and I could accomplish it merely by lying down. A week would be long enough. Then I'd get up, stretch, heat a can of frankfurters and beans over Rebel Shornicker's blow torch, rinse my face with a little water, then sit down and eat and talk again with Rebel about life in the Old South. Maybe the war would be over then, and I could think about going back to a rest area, and a cot, and PX rations, and a little room with a record player where I might find a record album of American music.

The path began to drop suddenly. There was a small valley below us. We took the road that followed the valley, the same yellow dirt road that we'd been on since we left the Appenines. We went up a hill about a hundred yards and sat down. There were young trees on the hillside: a small grove of them, just recently blossomed into new delicate green life. It looked like we'd never stop climbing hills. Mt. Belvedere had been an important stronghold for the Germans. The highway below it was a vital link between Florence and Bologna; Bologna was a key gateway to the Po Valley. Belvedere had resisted several assaults from Allied forces in the five months prior to December 1944. In January 1945 I arrived with the 10th Mountain Division in the port of Leghorn, Italy. I stood on the ship's deck with hundreds of other GIs and gazed on a calm, clear afternoon, at the rubble of ships in the harbor and the bombed-out buildings along the waterfront, and then heard for the first time the sound of war. In the distance, to the northeast, in the Appenine Mountains beyond Leghorn and Pisa, I heard the sound of artillery fire. It was a heavy, ominous sound. I knew at once the war was there, and I would have to face up to it. There on that ship a fear entered my brain and consciousness. It would not release nor free me until the war ended.

We disembarked and were trucked to a small mountain village south of Mt. Belvedere, called Prunetta, which had been by-passed by the German army. Here we engaged in daily, rigorous training for whatever lay ahead. Whenever we saw hills, we invariably climbed them. If there was a mountain in front of you, you climbed it, if you were a mountain man. John Muir once said: "The mountains are calling—I must go." Another mountaineer, named Marlow, asked why he risked his life on the sheer heights of mountains, said simply, "Because they are there." I, too, loved mountains, but now they were behind us, behind me, so I need not climb them again soon. If we went far enough north there would be more mountains to climb in Austria: the Dolomite Alps. And glaciers to cross, if we had to invade Germany from the south.

It was getting hot. We sat and looked down at the valley road and watched the trucks and men moving around. It was a beehive of activity down there. I suddenly decided to take a sunbath. I walked up to a patch of soft green grass, took off both my shirt and two undershirts, and lay down on my back and stretched my arms out to receive the sun. I had not indulged myself this way since I left basic training in northern Florida. God. Damn. But now the sun felt different: it felt really good. I started to drift off into a wonderful state of sleep. But Holman found me out. "Bassett, what in the hell do you think you're doing? This is not Miami Beach! Put your clothes back on and start digging!"

I unfolded my shovel, screwed it up tight at a forty-five degree angle, dropped to my knees and started chopping away at the earth. The soil went down six inches and then gradually turned into rock. We all gave it up, one by one, and no more was said about digging. The trees provided little round areas of shade and we sat under them.

The company brass was gathered at the foot of the hill. They were all sitting down. They looked hot—tired. Like me, they looked like they were sick of it all . . . Bucher was examining a map with Lt. Pierranunzi and Sabin. Sgts. Orrell and Carafa were looking on, too. There were some boxes of grenades piled up. The squad leaders started passing them out. Each man got three. The grenades were each in black cylinders which were two separate sections, one inside the other. After you pulled off the yellow tape that kept the cylinders together, you pulled the cylinders apart, and there was your grenade.

We hated to get grenades again. Me especially. I had helped carry our first captain down from Mt. Belvedere the morning after we had captured it. I was still green. I still could not look a corpse in the face. I was in a delicate condition. Maybe I could stomach war, and maybe I couldn't. When Captain Luther was killed, I asked, "How did he die?"

I was told that he had raised a hand grenade and held it up by his head, ready to throw when a bullet hit the grenade and caused it to explode, killing him instantly. I was assigned with four others to carry him down the mountain to a great pile of frozen corpses a few hundred feet from the summit. Four GIs put him on a blanket and tried to carry him down, but the slope was steep and he kept falling off. I trailed dismally behind them carrying only his helmet. I could not go near him; I was still in a state of terrible combat shock. One of my sergeants yelled at me: Hey, Bassett—what are you doing? What are you carrying? What's your problem? Etc. . . . etc. I was unable to respond: I saw the dead captain fall off the blanket repeatedly. I followed the procession down to the pile of American corpses and put his helmet down on the snow a few feet away from the grotesque pile and turned quickly away. I was in deep shock and did not know what I would do next.

I climbed back up the mountain to my position in the rock and ice and snow and waited. There was no catharsis: I looked around me and waited through the hours for something to happen to me. I slept a little. When I awoke, I was better.

In a few minutes we were all loaded up with the new grenades and back on the road again. There were poplars along the road, and tall hedges. The land was luxuriant with vegetation. Beyond the hedges, round green hills rose above the homes that sat along the road. There was no sign of life there. The land was begging for care. Here and there along the shaded avenues leading to the houses were signs of the departed Hun: small camouflaged staff cars and trucks lying in burned confusion. We passed two dead oxen beside the road. They were monstrous creatures— white with wide curving horns. Their intestines were spilled out and swarms of black flies circled over them. They looked strangely pathetic with their eyes shut, sprawled in the dust. I could see in their faces the agony of death. Peters, a new replacement from the reppo-deppo, began to get sick to his stomach, and after he'd puked twice, he howled up to Holman that he was sick and that he was falling out. The oxen were too much for him.

We were coming to a small village. The line stopped suddenly and we moved off the road under some shade trees and lay down. We were near a school, a neat red brick structure shaded by a grove of tall poplars. I moved in by the school and lay down. The rest of the squad soon followed and presently we were all stretched out flat on our backs, our heads propped up on our helmets, enjoying the shade and the cool breeze that fanned the trees. Except for the terrific booming every so often of a heavy gun nearby, it was a very pleasant break. A flock of geese came waddling down the road. Some of the GIs were hooting at them and chasing them. Across the road there was a large stone church. It was a very beautiful building, undamaged thus far by the war. Our break grew into a long welcome rest. Some GIs began opening their C rations. I had some cereal and one can of meat and rice. It tasted good: just like the Spanish rice my mother used to fix.

Joe Yerchin, as was customary with him, began to look around to see what he could see and perhaps find what he could find. Joe was twenty-one, but he looked much older. I thought he was practical and shrewd. He knew all the time what the score was. I admired him a great deal. Now he poked his head into an open window of the school and said invitingly: "Come on, Bassett, let's take a look inside: we'll probably find something."

"No thanks, Joe," I said, "you go ahead. I'll stay out here."

"OK," he said. He had only asked, thinking I might be interested. Seeing that I wasn't, he made no attempt to persuade me. He boosted himself up and through the window and began prowling around. Jack Mathews, red-eyed and fagged out, lay on the back steps, sound asleep—his grease gun by his side. I was afraid there might be booby traps in the school. Whatever else I thought made no difference in my mind. Booby traps had the preference, and since booby traps spelled death, I said: no thanks.

After two hours had passed, two jeeps pulled up in front of the school. The men got out and looked around appreciatively. "This'll make a good Division CP," one said. Division CP eh? The division must be running pretty fast to find us here.

I woke Jack up: "Come on, Jack," I said, "the line's moving again." We hit the road. We went through the village, and I stopped briefly once beside a rather ornate altar erected beside the road in front of a house. It was covered with yellow dust, the linen draped over the altar was a dirty gray and the small vase of flowers still sitting upright was now a bunch of withered stems. A little farther on we passed two dead GIs lying on the edge of the road. They had not been dead long; their jackets were still green and their blood hadn't been covered by the dust yet. I would not look at their faces. Their rifles and two boxes of ammo lay where they had been dropped. It looked like a sniper had got them.

You are young and you are a fool, the voice of the road was speaking to me again, for this road will but lead you to your death. I shivered in the heat of the dusty yellow road. This time the voice had reached me. But again I shrugged it off for it was so very old and low and I already knew I would not drop out of the line of march unless I was wounded or killed. I marched on, caught up in the loose steady rhythm of combat boots hitting the road, kicking up the dust, carrying us onward, ever onward, to the Po.

Someone pointed at the hills to our left and yelled: "Hey look at the paisans up there!" There were about thirty of them sitting on a hillside. Some of them were waving big white flags.

"Yeah! Go on and wave, you no good fucking Guineas!" another yelled. 'Yeah, for all we know, you're Krauts in Guinea clothes!'' When I looked back one last time, several women were still waving their flags.

A 91mm mortar company began passing us on the right. They were going twice as fast as we were. We could see the beginnings of another town ahead. We watched it come closer and closer, and then we were starting to pass through it. Two shots rang out suddenly, followed by a short burst of fire. Sniper! We ran off the road into an open doorway and squatted down inside. Now and then the sniper would fire. It was difficult then because no one had an idea. Sabin was not there—nor was Carafa. No one spoke while we waited. There was nothing to say. I looked once at Sgt. Holman, but he was lost in his own thoughts as he peered out the doorway. Outside, two British tank destroyers suddenly pulled up. The two Limeys in the top turrets were wearing flat wool caps, like always. They didn't seem to have heard the sniper.

Holman yelled out to them: "Hey—hey!! Better get down; there's a Kraut machine gun firing at us!" They hastily ducked their heads. Then, in a minute, they had moved on. An old man walked slowly up the street. His look was vacant: he was beyond caring. I would have given him my rations, but I sensed he did not need food just then. A jeep roared down the road. Then the sound of running feet: the sound grew louder, and Sabin ran past the doorway.

He quickly returned and stopped at our doorway: "Holman: start getting your squad out of here—send two at a time—there's a hundred yard gap down the road: tell them to make it fast." I was the sixth one to go. The others were waiting by some buildings beyond a long open space. They rooted the rest of us on. I sprinted through clouds of dust, praying as I went, my eyes squinted nearly shut, gasping for breath, and collapsed on the road finally near a jeep.

"Get up, soldier," a voice commanded me. I looked up and saw Lt. Colonel Shelor standing by his jeep, looking down at me.

"Yessir," I said, scrambling to my feet. Colonel Shelor looked rugged standing there in the sunlight.

"Son," he said in his fine Southern accent, "we've got these bastards on the run: do not doubt that we will be victorious." I nodded and staggered over to where Holman stood beside a pile of bricks.

A strange captain came up to Rebel Shornicker and me then, and said he wanted us to go with him. He took us into one of the nearby buildings. He led us through a room to a back porch that overlooked a creek.

75

"Now, I want you men to stay here and watch that house there on the side of the hill—yes, the big square stone house. If you see any suspicious movements, tell me at once." We nodded. "I'll let you know when to leave." And then he left. The porch was narrow: four feet wide and twenty feet long. It was filthy. Dirty, cobwebbed dish pans and pots were stacked in the corners. Papers and long-discarded wine bottles with the Seal of Bologna littered the floor. At one end of the porch was a sink, two sections in the bottom thick with green slime: this too was filled with rusty cobwebby pans. On the single porch shelf there was a disorderly row of cans and bottles and little knicknacks used in the kitchen. It was all junk. The porch itself was about ready to collapse. Its walls were thin and poorly shingled and full of holes. The porch had three windows. I sat on the sink and watched from the end window. Rebel looked out of the middle one, and Okie, a farmer from Oklahoma, stood at the other window.

"Okie," I said, "are you a good shot?" He turned his blond weatherbeaten face towards me and grinned: "Yeah, I reckon I'm a fair shot."

"What'd you shoot in Oklahoma?"

"Well, when a red-tail hawk sailed over my chicken coop, if the air was calm, and he barely moved, I could nail that hawk maybe up to two hundred yards."

"Whee-ee-ew," I softly whistled. "That's mighty fine shooting."

"Yep," he said—"I had to protect my market. We was on hard times and every chicken and every egg brought food to my kids and my wife and me, and kept us goin'."

"Couldn't you have stayed on your place—why—

I'm sorry—I mean: did you have to join the Army and leave your family and the chickens?''

"Well—uh, no uh, well, I guess I did too. That is, I guess I did have to join the Army.''

"What in the hell for?'' I exclaimed.

"Shhh-h-h'' he whispered, looking carefully out at the hill. "Look there, three people coming out of the house and there they go into a big hole in the ground.''

"That's OK,'' I said. "That's their bomb shelter, so it's OK.''

"Whew!'' Okie passed his hand over his eyes and shook his head.

"Could you shoot a Kraut, Okie—like you'd shoot a hawk?'' Okie turned to look at me and I saw that he was very sad.

"Bass: you remember the films they showed us in Basic—the Why We Fight Films? Well, when I seen these films, I cried all through them and then I cried at night in my bunk, but I told no one. But I knew then I could shoot Hitler or one of his men, or all of his men. Yes, Bass, I can shoot a Kraut. Yes, and I was drafted. They told me that chickens could not feed the Army like wheat, or corn, or cattle or hogs, so they told me I must go and be a soldier—be brave—and fight for the sacred honor of my country. So I am here in Italy to kill Hitler's men.''

"Like me, Okie, like me,'' I said, "I'm here to kill Hitler's men also.''

The sniper had stopped shooting. I got tired of looking at the hill and the big stone house, so I went into what must have been the dining room. It was the only room on the ground floor that escaped damage. The shades were drawn, so the room was dark. I rummaged through some drawers and a cabinet, but

77

there was nothing of value. A few books and post-cards lay on a table. A baby carriage stood by the front door; there were two small quilts in it. The fireplace was dark and dismally cold. I picked up a small powder puff that lay on the mantle and sniffed it. A faint odor of violets still remained. I put it back on the shelf and went out to the porch again. Rebel cautioned me about looking directly out of the window because he had a great respect for the ability of Kraut snipers. We sat on the porch a little longer, and then we knew we'd been forgotten. No one came to relieve us. We were disgusted and left the building. Our company had left the village. We were told to hurry up and catch up with our platoon. Already it was twilight—another day gone by. Almost. We followed a path that went up a hill. Below, on the main road, the tanks opened fire with their .50 caliber machine guns, and cannons. As I walked, I saw small chunks of white earth under my feet with green blades of grass coming up. The dim, half light of ending day hung over the land. A vicious whirring sound passed over our heads and I turned to see a shell explode just above us. No one was hit. The path turned upwards. Another 88 came in and hit well above us. The .50 caliber tracers from tanks were chattering over our heads in a continuous stream. They were covering the hills beyond us with protective overhead fire. The tracers were red. Someone lay dead by the side of the path. Who was it? A guy named Tex, they said. Then we stopped. I sat down on a bank and looked around me. The sound of the machine gun fire beat on my head like hammers of the devil. A tank suddenly exploded below on the road: it was a mass of white flames. I could see the tracers plunking across the top of the bare hill ahead, plowing up the earth.

We were getting up pretty high for overhead fire. We moved on and came to a vineyard. On a nearby hilltop a shell set off a German flare and rocket dump. Orange, red, green flares and brilliant parachute lights: the whole thing went up. And then we were climbing again—fast. I looked up and saw someone lying beside the path.

"It's Jennings," someone said, "he's passed out." They were passing the word back then for a medic to come forward. God pity the poor medics, I thought, they could not be everywhere, especially in the mountains. If we had to use the beautiful black mules that came from Camp Hale, Colorado, how could medics follow the line of combat as well as the mules? Even the mules did not approach the lines of combat on the mountain tops of Italy.

Then we were in tall grass near the top. No one knew what to do. The platoons were all mixed up. Sergeant Miller was nearby. He didn't know where to put his platoon. Everyone wanted to know where Bucher was. I began looking for Holman and the second squad. I was told they were up by the house that sat alone on the hill. I walked around the house to a haystack and there was my squad. "Glad to see you," Holman said. "You'll sleep with Branche tonight. Come with me: I'll show you where to dig in."

There was no moon and the stars seemed to have disappeared. We could see nothing. Out in front was a great void. I had the feeling it was endless. Once or twice I caught the faint winking of a light. I had a strong suspicion that out there, hidden by the night, lay the fabled Po Valley.

Holman put us on the edge of the field: we started digging. We started slowly. The next thing I heard was the low pa-lomp of a mortar shell leaving the tube. A few seconds of silence, then a low whine that descended through the darkness with terrifying speed. Instantly Branche and I fell down and tried to jam ourselves in the hole that was only just begun. The shell seemed to graze the tops of our heads, and then we could hear its sound—the shuddering shoosh-oom as it went by and exploded somewhere below, out of sight. Now we moved into high gear and dug for China. We weren't half done when Holman arrived and told us to stop digging and return to the haystack. He said, in a very despondent, low voice: "We've taken the wrong hill. We've got to move to the next hill." I was very tired so I didn't say anything. My foxhole buddy, big Jim Branche, let out a long low whistle, but said nothing.

Holman spread us out below the house and told us to lie down until we had orders to move out. Finally, Capt. Bucher got the company organized and we started off again. There was a narrow ridge connecting the two hills. It was very still. We crossed the ridge and started up a long driveway. Sfft-Bang!— Crack! Crack! And then a short burst from a burp gun. Everyone hit the ditch. Word came back for the weapons to move up and set up in the field and to lay down fire on the houses just ahead. In a minute I saw "The Lens" Davis from Escanaba, Michigan. He wore thick lenses to correct his astigmatism, always cheerful, always dirty, always willing to carry his .30 caliber machine gun wherever it was needed. I saw him and his two helpers running along the top of the bank by the road. They moved in short, fast rushes. Presently they were firing. After a long burst, the Germans fired back. Then Davis opened up again. Rebel and I were lying close together. Right at our feet was the entrance to a German trench that wound around the brow of the hill. It appeared to be deserted. Holman told us to keep an eye on it. An idea slowly came to me: why not use it?

But was it dangerous? Could the Krauts sneak down in it from around the hill and ambush us here at the entrance? The heavy chattering of machine gun fire close overhead forced the decision upon me. I finally reasoned the safer thing to do was to get in the trench and hope to Christ the Germans didn't decide to use it. I began, reluctantly, to work my way in on my stomach. I got in and lay still and waited for something to happen. A little time passed. Above the trench I heard someone moving in the grass. The noise came closer . . . and a GI jumped over the edge into the trench.

"Son of a bitch!" he whispered. "I've had enough of that!" He lay down. I felt better now that someone else was between me and the rest of the trench. Then several more GIs crawled in and joined me. The trench was narrow so we lay more or less on top of each other. The war could go on indefinitely, I thought. We lay there a long time: I almost went to sleep.

As I began to drift off I heard someone calling my name: "Hey! Is Bassett in there? Hey Bassett, let's go; the 3rd platoon's moving out!" It was so damned comfortable and safe in that trench . . . but I guessed I'd have to go. I crawled over the others and out on the road and stayed crouched down. "Hurry up, Bassett, let's go—there's your squad up ahead." I half rose and ran and caught up with them. Ahead was a barnyard and a barn. Someone was standing by the barn door.

He opened it and looked inside, and then beckoned to us: "OK, let's go—go through to the other door and wait there for the signal to continue.'' Inside the barn I could see nothing. Wup! What was than? Oh, the barn was really a stable and I had brushed against the flanks of some cattle as we fumbled around in the dark. As we reached the other side I could vaguely make out their large white forms. At the door someone told us to leave, one at a time, run across a yard and then wait. We all made it safely. The shooting had stopped. We formed up and climbed up a steep bank, then another. Shrubbery appeared and then a house on top. More confusion. Everyone was mixed up. We sat on the steps leading to an open veranda. Above it was a beautiful white stone house. A pebbled path surrounded by elegant shrubs and cypress wound in and out of the garden. Some of the GIs were going into the house. I walked around the veranda and went into a hallway. GIs were walking around with lighted candles looking for something to eat. The house was deserted. It was too dark in there so I turned around and went back out.

In a little while the company was organized again and we were given areas to dig in. The 3rd platoon was put on the rear slope. Luca Luhaink and I were digging together. It was so steep there that we had to dig straight into the side of the hill. It became almost too difficult.

''Luca,'' I said wearily, ''let's see if we can do better elsewhere: we'll never get done digging here.''

''We can't go far Bass—you got an idea?''

''Let's drop down the hill a little.'' Suddenly Luhaink let out a low whistle: ''Hey Bass: look at what I found.'' I crawled down and nearly fell into a good-sized hole.

''Holy shit! A Kraut hole already dug!''

"Come on, let's not waste any time: let's try it for size." We got in and lay down.

"How about it, Bass?"

"Just about right, Luca; just a few inches more for our feet."

"Yeah, and it needs only a little widening out." But it was too easy. What if the hole belonged to a GI? What then?

"Luca," I said, "what if this belongs to one of ours?"

"It's tough shit if it does," Luca said as he dug mightily in the hole.

"OK," I said, "we'll pile the dirt up here in front—soon it'll look like we did it all." The hole was already chest high. What a stroke of good luck for us!

"Let's try it again, Bass." It still was too narrow. We stood up and saw Sgt. Branche coming towards us. He was looking all around him as he came.

"Oh-oh, if he says anything—this is ours." Branche came up to the hole and looked down at us:

"Hey, what are you doing? This is my hole."

"Naw," Luhaink said, "you must be mistaken: see all that dirt?" We continued shoveling out the dirt. But Branche was wise to us: he knew we'd taken his hole, but he wasn't sure how to say it. So he hung around—a little undecided—then he tried again:

"I still think you've got my hole. I've been out digging an OP, so, if you were considerate, you'd leave." That was one thing that Sergeant Branche had: he had manners, even up at the front. A pharmacist in civilian life, Branche moved painfully slow in the Army. His slowness was mistaken for cowardice by many, and there was a growing resentment against him. He continued: "You can't tell me you've dug all that deep in this short time."

We knew the jig was about up. Holman clinched it by coming up to us. "OK, Luhaink and Bassett, get out of there. I know myself this is Branche's hole. He's been digging an OP like he said—so scram!" I guess we hadn't expected Holman to stick up for Branche—but he had. Oh well, he had made him dig the OP when he knew that Branche had found the Kraut's hole.

My back ached and throbbed. My knees were raw and my hands were hot and blistered. We crawled back up to our original excavation and sat down dejectedly and looked out into the darkness. "Well, Bass," Luhaink muttered softly. "It didn't work."

"Don't I know," I moaned, "don't I know." We fell to the work without enthusiasm. I dug a row across, then moved forward far enough so my shovel would hit a least six inches in front of the row just dug. After I'd done about three or four rows, I sat back a minute and then scooped it out and packed it as best as I could around the edge. But the hill was so steep that most of each shovelful rolled down the hill. Then my eyes began to give out. I was staring at the dirt too hard. I dug for awhile with my eyes closed. I knew I was about finished. Luca agreed with me; it was time to quit. I put my raincoat under me on the dirt and used a sweater for a kind of pillow. The hole was too narrow. I took off my boots—even then my feet were right against the opposite end. The hole was very shallow, but we not longer cared. We were sweating when we lay down, and we were jammed together, and the ground was hard . . . and we slept.

I drifted fitfully into a long dream that began, painfully, with my first boy scout camping trip away from home when I was ten. I was brave at first; after all the camp was on the lake only fifteen miles from home. We were awakened early and told to run to the dock at the beach, naked, then run out the dock and jump into the lake. This I survived. There was an ornithologist there who told us he could talk with the birds. One afternoon I watched him make noises at a chickadee and saw the little bird almost leave the bush and fly down to his outstretched hand. The man called and called to the bird, but it did not leave the bush. I was very excited to see the man talking with the bird: it seemed he had the gift. Then different adults sent me on long wild goose-chases hunting sky hooks and shore lines. One morning I awoke with numerous welts on my hands and forearms. During the night, vicious crawling insects had bitten me, and now I was swollen and red and I itched terribly. I did not know what to do, so I sent a postcard to my mother and said I was not happy with camp and wanted to come home. The next morning there were more bites, and I grew more miserable. I sent another postcard and prayed mother would come and take me home. On the next day she came and when she saw my swollen hands she said I was going home. I hugged and kissed her fervently. She was not just my mother, she was also my angel who had rescued me. At home, my father listened to my account of the man talking to the chickadee.

"Jack," he said, "didn't you know that the chickadee is a most fearless bird—that only a little bacon or seeds are needed to bring them down to your shoulder and then to your hand?" I shook my head in disbelief.

The scene quickly changed: I found myself in the

rumble seat of a Model T Ford with Bernita. We were being chauffeured around the back roads above town by my high school classmate, Calvin. He said if Bernita would agree to be my date, he would drive us on a long romantic ride. It was 1943 and gas rationing was in full force, but Calvin and Baker and Odell had come up with enough gas ration coupons to keep the Model T running all night. Calvin gallantly drove us over cow paths and back roads at moderate speeds. He knew I had a terrible crush on Bernita, and was trying to help me as best he could. I had planned and waited for this moment for weeks. Bernita, smiling and demure, had accepted my invitation for a date in the Model T. Now we sat together in the dark as the night breeze whirled around us. I sensed she was waiting for me to say or do something, but I could only sit. I did not know what I should do. Then Bernita found a big white bed sheet on the floor. Gaily, she lifted it up and fluffed it out and put it over our heads. It fell down over us and our heads were close. She laughed and pushed up at the sheet. The right moment had come. I laughed and pushed the sheet up a little. The Model T sped on; Calvin did not look back at us, and then, carefully, she removed the sheet and put it back on the floor.

April 20, 1945

THERE WAS SOMETHING HOT, AND IT WAS BEATING on my face. I got warm, squirmed, and woke up. I looked down at my shirt: there was dirt on it and ants crawling around. The sun was up, and it was already a warm, clear morning. The bright light hurt my eyes. Everything was in color, like Sunday afternoon at the movies when the feature film opened in beautiful technicolor. The dirt in our foxhole was a warm orange-brown. I looked at my legs: they were partly covered by crushed green blades of grass.

I had to get up; it was already too hot. Luhaink was awake. We put up two sticks and spread a raincoat over them at the head of the trench to provide a little shade. Below the hill we could see our tanks moving up towards us. One came along the top of the hill and stopped near us by a hedge. A second tank pulled under some trees further away. An 88 came in—and another—and then another. The third shell exploded ten yards above our hole. We hit it and stayed face down. The Germans, of course, had seen the tanks. A few more 88s came in and the tanks slowly rumbled away. And the shelling stopped.

Since I had awakened, I was half aware that the Po Valley was just beyond the hills we occupied. Once or twice I got up and took a quick look. I saw, more than anything, a wide land stretching out east and west and north. It was all a beautiful green, dotted with small white houses, and with neat orchards and vineyards. I did not know how I felt, but I hoped that it was going to be a little better. I was excited at the prospect of going down there. Won't it be something, I thought, to be able to discover it all for myself?

They were getting water over by the house so I grabbed my canteen and went to find some. The pebbled path went past the house out to the edge of the hill. The well was there. The place was swarming with GIs filling their canteens and helmets. Over in the valley to the northeast a large city lay in the golden morning sun, suffused with a white mist that had not yet left the earth.

"Well, I guess that's Bologna."

"Yeah, can't be more than five miles away."

"Pretty quiet down there."

"Yeah." We stood and gaped at Bologna and the Po. I couldn't get enough of it. It was so fresh, so sparkling, so green. I imagined a rich perfume rising from those distant fertile fields: honeysuckle, roses, apple, pear and peach blossoms.

About noon we got orders to move out. We dropped down on a narrow dirt road and then began climbing again. It was hotter. No breeze. The sun beat on my steel helmet and so I sweat again. Up ahead on top of another round green hill was a large square stone building and beyond it another white house. There were trees all around the house, shading it from the sun. Sabin told us to move to the rear of the box-like building and sit down. But before I could fall to the earth, Sabin told me I was pulling an hour of guard duty. "Follow me, Bassett," he said.

"OK, sir," I replied. We filed through a grove of

tangled trees and stopped beside a deep hole that looked like a cave in the side of the hill.

"See those houses down there? Just keep an eye out for any suspicious movements. I'll send a relief out for you." He left. There were some old rags lying inside the entrance. It smelled bad. Flies buzzed around and flew in and out of the opening. Everything seemed calm and peaceful so I lay down a few feet away from the hole and tried to relax. I was thirsty and hungry so I opened a light dinner unit, took out the six crackers and laid them to one side. Then I pulled out my canteen and cup from the pouch and poured the cup nearly full. The orange powder I dumped in the cup and stirred with the large messkit spoon I always carried in my shirt pocket. Finally I emptied four small packets of Domino cane sugar in and stirred the whole works, and then settled back to enjoy it. The hard candies would be last. I looked down at the houses occasionally. What a pleasant afternoon it had become.

I was lying on my side resting when I heard above me a sputter and a cough and then three more short coughs. I looked up just as a P-47 nosed sideways and started falling. As it turned over I saw the pilot bail out and fall, his parachute streaming up at first in a thin white wriggle and then billowing out. The Thunderbolt crashed nose first below me in an earth-shaking collision. The pilot landed safely. Sabin and Carafa ran down the hill to rescue him. In a few minutes, they came up through the trees past me. The pilot was walking between Sabin and Carafa. The sweat was rolling down his forehead, but I could see that he was happy. The rest of the hour passed quietly and I was relieved. The platoon was in the barn trying to get some sleep in the cow stalls. Each stall was filled with hay. I found an empty stall and fell into a mound of soft yellow hay. I rolled over on my back and took off my boots. No hotel in the world, I thought, could be finer. Sleep, however, would not come. The barn was hot. It made me irritable and restless. Scores of black, medium-sized flies found me, landed on my bare feet and persisted in trying to fly up my nose.

Rumors started when General Hays pulled up in his jeep outside the barn. He disappeared, but his driver stayed in the jeep and told us we were being relieved soon, maybe that night, by the 86th Regiment. The stable became uproarious with laughter. I tried to join in and believe that it would come true— but I fell back quickly into the hay and just listened to all the wild talk and wondered if any of it was going to happen. The hay made me itch so I picked up an empty C ration can and went out to the well for a drink.

Above the hills south of Bologna I saw large white clouds of smoke, then came the ominous heavy boom-boom-boom of artillery. A faint rattling reached my ears as I stood transfixed by the distant evidence of battle. Machine guns too? But of course. The Germans were putting up a tough fight for the gateway to the Po. Bologna itself was peaceful. I shrugged it off as best I could. I sat down in the grass near other GIs, but the sounds of artillery were as the violent beating of my heart. Though I was not physically involved in that conflict, yet, in my mind, I was running wildly for a wall to protect me. I was aiming my rifle at a running Kraut; I was crying because my foxhole buddy had just been reported killed by a mine. I jumped up, realizing that the battle, for me, was from within.

In the middle of the afternoon, word came down that we were moving out again. There was no relief for us: the rumors had been false.

At 4:30 we formed up outside the barn and then moved out. We walked very slowly. We approached still another large white house and then followed a road around it. As we moved away I heard the sounds of a piano. The tones came out soft and clear to me. I imagined a child sitting at the keyboard, perhaps a boy, as I was once: eager to learn, eager to be able to play beautiful music. The music gradually died away.

I looked at the setting sun and the hills and found in their obvious beauty an unwillingness to enjoy it. Then I heard the sound of the marching feet, of my feet, and I knew we were going to fight the Germans again. I did not know where or when, but I knew it was ahead of us, down the long dusty road.

I glanced back at our column and saw that the word was being passed up. About fifteen men back, I heard what it was. We had lost contact with the weapons. Without the machine guns and BARs we were helpless, so we had to stop. Bucher held it up and we sat down to wait for the word to come up again. We sat there ten minutes and then I saw the men turning their heads and relaying the new word along the line. "The weapons are in sight."

"All right, men: let's go." Bucher led us off the road and started down an open field that began the gradual descent into the Po Valley. A gully opened up before us. It widened and deepened as we progressed. As we wound through a vineyard, there was a loud report from beyond the small round hills to our left front. The report, the searing zing of the shell through the air, and the explosion, all occurred in the

91

same breath. The shell hit smack in a column of troops across the gully. We stopped instantly. Through the noise of the explosion we heard agonized screams. Black smoke swirled crazily up from the tall green grass through the trees and blotted out the GIs in its midst. The column kept moving on down the hill—but now at a run.

Then another loud report—the almost simultaneous shriek of the shell and its short termination of flight on the green hillside—this time 50 yards below the column. Shrapnel from the explosion flew across the gully and sprinkled the side of the hill just below us. As it hit, small puffs of gray dust arose. The shrapnel had a terrific force. We stood on the edge of the hill and watched with mixed emotions. The line was stopped. There were no orders to take cover, or to start digging in. It was hairy. Some GIs around me were cursing. Others were demanding that the line move. Impatient demands . . . curses hurled at the empty air. More shells came in: they all landed across the gully. The line suddenly snapped into action. We trotted feverishly for several hundred yards down the side. The shelling stopped. Then we were going through a field of tall grass, heading straight for the Po.

"Watch out for snipers ahead," the word came back and kept on going back. We carried our M1s at port arms and watched some houses just ahead with intently staring eyes. The air was now a rose-tinted gray. There was only the afterglow of sunset hanging over us. The line weaved in and out of a small group of buildings at the edge of the field. We zeroed in on the open second story windows. I had a tingling sensation in my scalp. But there were no shots fired: the buildings were silent. We were in the Po Valley now.

I looked back and I could see the hills slowly receding as we went further into the new land.

Down a slanting road was a small town. The line turned left at the only intersection. It was wide there. The fields stretched away from the town to the north. An MP stood there, giving directions. We were in a hurry. The village was a vague blur. A double line of Kraut prisoners came towards us on the other side of the road. They had their hands behind their heads and were moving at a fast gait. Most of them wore their snug long-brimmed caps and long green overcoats. There was one GI close behind them with a carbine. He was not enjoying his detail. It was getting steadily darker.

The line turned off the road and into a grove of trees. Large, dark, cathedral-like, the interlaced treetops formed the intricate network of a roof overhead. We sat down under the black canopy of trees and night and waited once again for the familiar signal. A couple of GI ambulances moved in slowly with their lights off. Once there was the sound of running feet—the metallic clattering of hobnailed boots, probably Kraut prisoners being run back to a stockade. Some of them were jeering and shouting: they sounded rough.

Every so often there was the high softly swishing whistle of a Kraut shell that came from out in the Po. I could not be certain when or where they exploded. How strange to be on flat land again. The night was warm and soft and quiet. I had no feeling of danger. I sat on the ground and waited with an ever increasingly vacant stare. I was really becoming attached to the place when the signal was finally given. We moved out fast. The line went across the road and continued in a northwest direction through a field. Halfway across the field we stopped. There was something about the weapons or the troops behind us losing contact. Penny and Holman were sent for. They came back and said the company was digging in for the night. Each platoon was to have a certain area. Included in the instructions was an OK for each platoon to move into a house if they could find one close by. It was a black, black night. I could barely make out Holman as he stood filling us in. I could feel the tall grass around my knees, but could not really see it standing up.

Holman led us past a row of trees to a new field. "OK, Luhaink and Bassett; you two dig a foxhole here at this corner. Make it wedge-shaped. Baldwin and Devine are over there under that row of trees. Lopez and Whitey are in front of them. Penny and I are going over to that farmhouse to your right front and see if we can sleep there. If anything happens, we'll be right out." Holman and Sgt. Penny took off and we started digging. From time to time we would cease digging and listen. We were scattering the soil out wide. In case of trouble, a trench that had no ridge of dirt around it would be very difficult to see. We dug along fairly well. I took off my pistol belt, rifle, and raincoat and laid the M1 on the raincoat over on the opposite side—Luhaink's half of the trench.

Somewhere out in the dark to our front we heard voices. They were plainly audible but too far away to be understood. It sounded like arguing. "Hey, John T.: listen!" Luhaink spoke softly, but his tone was urgent. "Don't they sound like Krauts to you?" I strained my ears to hear, but could make nothing of it.

"Naw, Luca: don't you remember? Baldwin and

Devine and Lopez and Whitey are right out there under those trees to our front. Could be them talking.'' I had not convinced myself. The voices died down so we continued digging, scattering the soil with every shovelful. I had my half of the trench long enough to lie down in. Another shovel length across and I could quit.

A few more minutes passed, and then we heard a clanging sound—more of a rattle bang—like a pail being kicked over.

''Hear that, John T.?''

''Yeah, Luca, sounded like someone tripped over a pail, or something.''

''We better be more quiet.'' We stopped talking and began digging a little faster. We also looked more intently out in the blackness to our front. I could follow the furrows a little way; the earth was strangely light, and then I could see no further.

Suddenly, we heard the tail end of a series of ''Halts!'' yelled one after the other, fast. I was standing in the hole and facing the row of trees where Baldwin and Devine were digging. Then the crackling sound of rifle fire and of bullets snapping overhead and the sound of fast-running feet. It was the Krauts and they were rushing Baldwin and Devine and shooting as they came.

I was truly naked: my M1 was still lying on my raincoat opposite Luhaink. I fell down in the trench and hugged the ground and waited desperately for whatever was going to happen next. It happened that Luhaink's gun was beside him and he stood up and blazed at someone. I yelled at him: ''Luca! Throw me my gun!'' He reached over quickly and grabbed my M1 and I got up and took it and then joined him in firing straight out into the fields in front of us. The incoming bullets had a sharp stinging sound as they whacked through the air overhead. Then we heard someone running through the grass towards us. Closer and closer he came, and then he fell, moaning horribly, and thrashed around, and then lay still. The moaning continued together with his gasping for breath and mumbling in German.

There was no more shooting after that. The other Krauts ran away. The wounded Kraut kept making noises and then yelling loudly. I figured he was pleading with his comrades to come back for him. There was little we could do. We could not kill him: he was no longer a threat to us. But if we approached him in the dark he could still be dangerous. Holman and Sgt. Penny and the BAR man, Crest, came running out to us then.

"What happened?" Holman asked Luca.

"Oh, some Krauts rushed us. We got one over there in the grass, wounded. We better see if he's still able to shoot, and get his gun."

"Are Baldwin and Devine alright?"

"Yeah, I guess so."

They walked around the German cautiously and managed to grab his pistol. He started moaning for "Wasser—Wasser." But no one gave him water.

"Luhaink: you come with us. Bassett: you and Crest get over here in this grass and watch the field. The other Krauts may be hiding out in the grass." Crest went in the field a little way and lay down on his stomach. I followed and sat down a few feet from him. It was very wet there in the grass. The dew was falling like a light misty rain. It was tiresome sitting there straining to see all around in the dark. The excitement had passed. The Krauts would never return. The fanatical fire was gone from their hearts now.

They were separated and cold and would be glad enough to surrender in the morning. I finally had enough and told Crest I was going to find Penny and ask to be relieved. I found him in a hole under the row of trees. He told Luhaink to go with me to the house for an hour's break. Crest was left alone in the field to watch the wounded Kraut.

We found the house and went inside. The large front room was empty except for a man, his wife and their baby, sleeping on a mattress against the far wall. To the left, a door opened into the kitchen. It was lighted by two electric ceiling bulbs. All the kitchen windows were shut and covered with blankets. It was a large room, covered with mattresses. Lopez, Devine and Rebel were sleeping there. I became aware of a low humming sound. I looked harder and realized the room was full of flies. They were buzzing around the two lights, crawling up and down the walls, over the mattresses and the sleeping GIs, and all over the food that was spread on the table. I lay my rifle down on one of the mattresses and then lay down beside it. I put both arms over my face to discourage the flies and slept a little. Luhaink woke me up. I grabbed my rifle and sat up. We were joined by Rebel and Devine. After a careful look into the barnyard, we left the house quietly. We passed the long low brick barn. The night was still ink black. We found the path and headed out into the fields. As we approached Luhaink's and my original hole, up jumped Holman in the hole and put his rifle to his shoulder and pointed it across the path.

"Hoist der hand! Up! Hoist der hand!!" he shouted.

And almost under our feet a German soldier rose

up and raised his hands and muttered unbelievingly, "Mein Gott."

"Good God Almighty!" Holman gasped, "he's been creeping up on me for the last fifteen minutes. I couldn't see him, but I could hear him moving through the grass."

I was so shocked I could not move. The soldier was disarmed and taken back to the house by Penny and Devine. Rebel and I were put in Baldwin and Devine's hole under the row of trees. Rebel had been sleeping in the house when the Krauts attacked us, so when the wounded Kraut began moving a little and said "Wasser—Wasser," Rebel picked up his M1 and fired two shots at him before I could stop him.

"Hey! Rebel! Hey!" I yelled. "For Christsake—stop! He's already wounded! Don't shoot him up any more!" Rebel apparently did not hit him because no sound came from the tall grass. The next hour passed without further incident. I was relieved and returned to the house. I went into the kitchen and there was the Kraut who had surrendered an hour ago. He was sitting in a chair facing the door. Penny was sitting at a table on his right, his grease gun in front of him. Mooney sat behind him with a rifle in his lap. I put down my helmet and rifle and sat on a mattress.

"Can he speak English, Penny?" I asked.

"Yes, he said something when he came in, but hasn't said a word since." I sat and looked at him. He was middle-aged: light gray hair combed back smoothly from a pale brow. Deeply lined face, an air of complete resignation, of supreme exhaustion. He sat and stared steadily at the door. I knew I would not sleep, so I sat on the mattress and talked with Penny. Penny was ready to fall asleep. I thought maybe talking might help him stay awake.

"What rank would you say he is—lieutenant?" I asked Penny.

"Yes, his shoulder insignia looks like it." I leaned back and put my hands under my head so I could watch him too. He put his hand in his pocket and very calmly drew out a round black cylinder. For a second I felt an alarming flutter, realizing that my rifle was up beside the door. Penny didn't show any interest. The German opened the cylinder and gazed at something inside it for a minute and then carefully put it back in his pocket. I knew he was looking at a photo of his family. Yes, he had, by a miracle, survived. Now it was over for him. If only his family had survived too. Then, perhaps, there was hope for the future.

Penny was nodding. His head slowly inched over until it almost dropped. Then his head snapped back up again. I watched him repeat the performance over and over again. The prisoner did not seem to notice; he sat very still with his legs crossed, sat up very straight—not stiffly—but as though it were an old habit. Penny finally gave it up and put his head on the table and slept. Mooney was awake though. I lay back and put my arms over my face to keep the eternally hovering, crawling flies off my face.

It was Christmas time at the service club at Newport News. We were at our APO waiting for the order to line up and climb aboard a ship destined for Europe. We had heard it would be Italy, but no one knew anything so we moped around the base and I found some comfort in milling around the club with the other GIs who would be sailing with me, and watching the pretty civilian hostesses as they offered coffee and cake to every GI possible and smiled and made small talk. I sat down in a corner and my thoughts turned to my home in upstate New York. What time was it? Nine o'clock. At home, Mom would still be wrapping a few presents. Dad would be half-asleep in his big chair with a half-empty bottle of beer at his finger tips. My sisters, Alta, Lois and Betty would be gathered in front of the piano. Betty would be playing Christmas carols on the piano, and Lois and Alta would be playing their flutes. Soon the flutes would be put down and the three of them would be singing all the familiar songs while outside the house snow would be falling, a perfect white Christmas.

April 21, 1945

It was too painful to bear any longer—I woke up. Penny was removing one of the blankets over a window. There was a light grayness outside now. It would be light when I went out on guard. Time to go: rifle and helmet and bandoliers. Since it was light, Penny put only one GI in each foxhole. I went out to the hole Luca and I had dug. Everything was a light gray. The fields were wet with dew. There was the plowed field behind me, some houses at the far end, a vineyard to the right; the path, the row of trees and the field of tall grass to the front. And there, all sinuous and silvery, where the grass was flattened still, was the path the Kraut lieutenant had made when he was creeping up on Holman. Out in the middle of the field lay a dead Kraut. I thought it must be the one Luca had shot at first. I knew I had not shot him. I had simply fired into the night: I had seen no one running. I had not zeroed in on a target. I felt no remorse. I did not care. Everything was serene. The fog was slowly lifting. Our hole was damp, but not muddy. I sat on the edge of the hole and looked around. The wounded Kraut still lay in the grass a few yards away. Mooney came walking out later with his carbine. "Hiyuh—say, know where I might be able to pick up anything?"

"I don't know—there's a dead Kraut out there in the field. No one's picked him yet." I was sure he was dead. His position cinched it; he was lying bent over with his face in the grass. He was dead alright. Mooney was a little hesitant, but he went out to check anyway. He bent low over the German, then straightened up quickly. He took nothing.

The German in the grass was still alive. Baldwin came over to him and gave him some water. Another GI lit a cigarette for him. I could see him lying there, one arm sticking up, holding a cigarette. Baldwin was carrying a small yellow leather holster on his belt, with the pistol still in it. I was curious to see him so I left the hole and walked over. "Hey, Baldy," I said, "where'd you get the gun?"

"Off the German lieutenant. The captain over there said I could keep it." The Kraut in the grass was lying on his back. He was a bloody mess. The true fanatic type, I thought: he had a large thick head, big bulky body. I looked at his face, especially his eyes. I could see him as he came running toward us, like a wild savage from the distant past, his facial muscles distorted by hate and rage. Now, however, his face was blank. His eyes were a dark gray and wild with pain, his hair bushy and dark. His face was plain white with thick lips. He said nothing but looked at each of us in turn. Had I wounded him, I thought quickly? Did I hate him now? Did I pity him? Should he be nursed back to health? Wouldn't he have killed me if I were lying there instead of him? I stared back at his pain-filled eyes and then looked away.

"He's really shot up, isn't he?" I said to Baldwin.

"Yeah. Been wounded five times at least." Two of his fingers had been shot off. There was blood on his legs and all over his chest. The man was exceptionally strong, but how long would he live?

The light over the field was brighter. The sun would be up soon.

I saw Sgt. Johnson coming across the field with three German soldiers. They stopped in front of us while Johnson searched one of them: a corporal. I watched him go through the corporal's little personal bag. He was very fast, yet methodical. I asked him something, but he did not answer. I should have known better: not while he was digging for the spoils of war in a little bag. The three of them were teenagers: tall, blond, athletic, clean cut, good-looking Nazis. They smiled at me. I almost forgot and smiled back, but caught myself in time and looked down at the grass. But of course—the answer flashed through my brain. They were unharmed, and for them, the war had just ended. After a while they could go home.

They had brought two poles and a kind of sack, tied in the middle, for a stretcher. They had come to carry the wounded German over to the POW camp. The makeshift stretcher looked flimsy. After a little, they walked over to the wounded German. Two took hold of his arms, and the corporal his legs: they lifted him and put him quickly down on the stretcher. He groaned and his body tightened up with pain. They got ready and began to raise it. When he was a foot off the ground, the poles threatened to snap, so they had to let him back down.

Someone came out and told us to report back to the house. We were moving out again. The courtyard was full of people: cousins, aunts, nephews, daughters, uncles, grandparents had come to see us, the brave American liberators. They all seemed friendly, and one filled my canteen for me. There was a small pile of Kraut rifles in front of the door. I went inside. Lt. Sabin was sitting in the kitchen eating a bowl of bread and milk. It looked very good to me, but when I saw the swarms of flies around him, I quickly lost my appetite. I withdrew. Sabin appeared soon afterward and checked over the platoon and got us ready to shove off.

But first we had to eat. Sabin took us down a path and then crossed the field toward a red brick house surrounded by a lawn and shrubs and trees. I Company was there, sitting around and eating C rations. A group of German prisoners was sitting on the lawn twenty yards away watching the men eat. We were famished. Holman called us to him and gave us our C rations. We were given three heavies each.

The sun was up at last, shedding golden light across the green grass. It hurt my eyes so I went around to the rear of the house, in the shade, and sat down and ate my cold ham and egg ration. Somewhere out in the fields I heard the chatter of a machine gun. Although it sounded fairly close, no orders were given, no one moved, we just kept on eating. The noise made me nervous, but I watched my buddies closely. They all sat impassively eating. Must be having some trouble out there with another band of Krauts.

A young woman came walking slowly across the field to the house with her infant son. He was naked except for a brown sweater that came down to his navel. For you, too, I thought, little one, the war has ended. Your mother and you are unharmed. The Po Valley will feed you better now, and I pray you will never grow up and have to fight in a war. . . .

Captain Bucher yelled at the company and gave us the order of march and we moved out. On the way I saw the badly wounded German lying among the other prisoners in the shade. I kept on looking at him as we left. He lay still, a dark gray hulk on the ground. He was expendable, I thought; when he came screaming across the field at us, he was already committed to his death. He had not stopped us, nor hurt us. It was the fortunes of war. His comrade had died. He still lived. For him, too, the war was over, and he might go home again. Or he might not.

I jerked my head back around and put the scene out of my mind. We went out on a road, a white dirt road. There were farms everywhere: they all looked alike. For each farm there was a large square area of land devoted to growing fruit trees, grapes, or row crops. At one corner of each farm lived the owner in a large square brick house. We marched from the southeast corners to the north or northwest corners.

Then back on the road again. We kept a steady pace. Along the road everything was coated thickly with white dust. Even the nearby landscape was bleak. The green of the grass and foliage seemed to have faded. We passed an overturned truck lying in the ditch; only the blackened frame was left and still smoking. The line stopped infrequently, and I squatted down or sat on the road the few minutes we had to wait. There were deep holes dug on both sides of the road. The Krauts had used them as observation posts. To the left, a few feet from the road, a dead Kraut lay in his green uniform under a tree, rotting in the shade. Flies buzzed around the corpse. I held my breath until I was well past it.

"You're a fool, a fool, a fool." The ancient voice of the road was reproaching me again. "For this road will but lead you . . . !"

"Yes!" I said aloud angrily, "to my death."

Luca turned around in front of me: "What did you say, John T.?"

"I'm talking to the road, Luca."

"What in hell's the matter with you?"

"Nothin'. I'm pooped. I just said I'd—I'm fed up with this fucking road!"

Ahead there was a large grove of trees and tall grass all around, sometimes as high as my pistol belt. Through the grove, and through more groves down the road, and through the long hot spring day into the Po. We passed several Limey artillery units. Big cannons deployed among the trees, covered with camouflage nets; the men sitting around in their undershirts taking it easy; one crew sitting around a fire while one was cooking some beef in a pot; a delicious aroma came out to greet us as we passed by. I saw white bread too. There were more groves, but only one road. A P-47 suddenly swooped down and roared over our line. Sabin threw himself into the ditch. But he was the only one. He got up quickly and back on the road again.

Then it was sunset and the column ahead was winding through another grove of trees. Every so often there was a faint crack that came from beyond the hedges and trees along the road. I wondered if there was a sniper hidden out there taking pot shots at the column. My squad ended up in a long narrow grassy field in the center of the grove. It was time to lie down.

"I'm going to sleep, John T." Luca said. "If we move again, wake me up." I grunted and remained standing. I didn't feel like lying down because the field was all tall coarse string stalks and there were big black ants crawling around, and then the line might start moving again and it just wouldn't do to lose I Company. So I sat down on my pack and hoped I looked inconspicuous in the grass. Luca began to snore. It was getting dark. GIs were coming out of a big barn across the field with bales of hay. The line started off without warning. I ran over to Luca and pushed him.

"Come on, Luca, the line's moving. Let's go!" I said.

"Humph-grmmph!" Luca woke up with a jerk and threw himself together. The rest of the squad came too. We fell in with our company. The line moved about one hundred feet and then stopped. Everyone sat down again. Hurry up and wait. Then the word came back that we were right there for the night. I unwrapped my raincoat and put it on, buttoned it all the way up and turned up the collar. It would serve as mattress and blanket. I lay down against a small bank, my left hip on the level ground and the rest of me up against the bank. I put my helmet on and lay down. The ground was hard. I was pooped. I slept and dreamed fitfully.

Why, why it was Christmas Eve, that most magical, wonderful night of the year. But where was I? I was not home with my family. No, I was alone this time. I was in the Army. I was at a P.O.E. at Newport News, Virginia, waiting to be shipped overseas. I was waiting in the service club, listening to Christmas carols and writing a letter to my mother. A small group of GIs was standing a few feet away. I overheard them talking about one of my favorite radio and movie stars, Red Skelton. One said he had heard that Skelton was going to appear at the service club within the hour. I quickly folded up my writing kit and stood up and stepped close to the group. They were very excited by the news. I caught the excitement too, and

107

when they moved away, I followed them. We went down a back hall to a dark, unmarked door. They opened it and entered, and I with them. The room was large. There was a little stage at the far end. Folding chairs filled half the room. A few GIs were already sitting down in the room. It was semi-dark with one ceiling light over the stage and two red exit lights over doors on the left and right of the stage. The room was charged with anticipation. I sat down and waited. More GIs came into the room and sat and whispered among themselves. I looked around and saw that perhaps thirty or forty GIs were sitting behind me.

Then a GI came onto the stage from the back. He was a technical sergeant. He came up to the stand-up microphone and adjusted it, cleared his throat, and in an emotional voice said: "Tonight, you are privileged, as I am, to welcome a fine talented and patriotic American citizen to this place—right here to this room. I have known this man for years. We were friends before he became famous. Fellow men: it is my distinct honor to present to you Red Skelton!!" With that, three overhead spot lights came on and lighted up the stage. There was a moment's delay. The sergeant ran back into the dark. I heard several low voices and the sounds of a door opening and closing. Then out he walked, under the spot lights. He looked exactly as he had in his most recent movie: tall, dressed in GI fatigues, his red hair somewhat rumpled, and a big infectious grin on his face. He acknowledged the introduction of the sergeant and confirmed that they were old and dear friends. Then he fell instantly, easily into his first routine. I was already seated in the front row, but there were fifteen feet between me and the stage. I half rose and scooted my chair forward another eight feet. I was then as close to Red Skelton as I dared to be. A table was brought out, and several bottles and glasses.

He pretended to be a bartender who knew it all. He picked up a shot glass and poured liquor into it and then into a tall clear glass. He picked up another bottle and poured it into the same glass until it was full. Then he could not remember what he had done. So he took a long swizzle stick and mixed up the concoction with strong swirls. Then he lifted the glass to his lips and drank.

"Smoo—oo—ooth—thh—!!" Skelton gurgled uncertainly. He slipped and nearly fell. He grabbed at the table, knocking over two bottles, and managed to get his elbow on the table and stood back with a slaphappy smile on his face. The room roared with laughter. I was laughing so hard I could not breathe.

April 22, 1945

I WOKE UP LAUGHING AS I FELT A STICK SMACK against my feet. "Come on, Bassett, wake up! We'll be on the road soon." Holman was waking up his squad with a tent pole. It was clear and very cold. Over on the road GIs were waiting for the C rations to come. A jeep had been bringing them up to us every day. There were two tanks parked just off the road. It was hard as hell to find anything to lean against. All the trees in sight, every bank and both sides of each tank had GIs leaning against them. Four for five GIs were lying on a pink and rose quilt on a bank under the trees where the sun now shone.

The jeep came and the rations were dumped on the road. The driver said there was a rumor that we were going to try for the Po River, and that trucks were waiting up ahead to take us there. I sat shivering in the dirt, eating cold meat and beans with my big soup spoon, and thought what a crock of shit that was. Then I remembered the long ride on the trucks that carried us from Prunetta to the base of Mt. Belvedere. And when it grew dark, we crept up and down hills with the headlights off until we stopped on a narrow road and disembarked. In spite of myself, I began to get a little excited. I got up and threw the slimy food away and got my gear in shape. And just in time. Bucher ordered the company to form up, and in another five minutes we were heading back to the road.

Down the road and under the trees I saw the tail end of a truck. Then I saw a line of trucks. My mouth fell open—my heart beat faster. It happened quickly. We hopped on. At last, we rode. We traveled along beautiful black-top roads that wound through fields, followed narrow canals passing beneath long rows of slender poplars, waving and billowing in the fragrant morning breeze.

We began to enter a village, but the trucks all stopped suddenly. Instinctively we smelled danger and piled helter-skelter out of the trucks. As we did so we heard machine gun fire up ahead. We ran for a house on the other side of the ditch.

We ran into a workshop. There, puttering around on his workbench, was a big, blue-eyed Italian. He wore a battered brown hat. His face was red, wrinkled and cheerful.

"Bon giorno—welcome—bon giorno," he said, and then turned back to his work. It seemed to be just another day's work for him. I could see no sign of apprehension in his face. Outside we could hear the bullets cracking between the workshop and the residence across the yard. Both were of stone. No one said anything for a few minutes. We knew the Kraut fanatics had set up a couple of machine guns down the street to kill as many as they could, the real purpose being to slow us up—to give their army more time to escape across the Po, into the Alps of Austria.

Let them have their fun; the stone walls were the sort of protection we should be strong enough to carry on our backs. Outside, a machine gun section was slowly working its way up to the house. Poor boys, they had a rough deal out there, having to stalk those crazy Krauts. The big blue-eyed Italian was still smiling. He probably knew the Germans were there all the time.

There was a stairway in the rear of the shop. Odds and ends hung from the ceiling and junk was piled up in the corners. I sat on the stairway and listened to the racket. Some GIs went into the house across the yard: they wanted to see if they could locate the machine guns. There was another little room adjoining the workshop, partitioned into three compartments, probably for calves or hogs. High up one wall there was a small rectangular door. A ladder leaned against the end of the room. I was curious. I picked up the ladder and put it under the door and climbed up. I unlatched the little door and opened it. There, on a roost, sat a great white turkey. It was dark in there but the turkey was awake. It turned its head and stared coldly at me. "There there, Mister Tom," I said softly. "No need to be alarmed: I'll not give you away." I shut the door softly and climbed back down.

Back in the shop I saw the Italian had brought out some wine and everyone was having a drink. The bottle was very tall and dark green. I poured some into my cup. It was a dark red and barely cool. Its taste was soothing, comforting. Were we not a fine group of redblooded American soldiers, I thought? Each of us potential heroes? If Sabin or Carafa were seen coming for us, we might have taken the wine and run for it—to safety—that's it—to a safe place where we could rest and drink while the noise and pain of battle floated gently past us forever. Then the shooting stopped. It was very quiet in the workshop. We stood around and drank some more wine.

"Come on, boys," Sergeant Orrell motioned to us,

"let's go: they're reorganizing." I took a last gulp and ran out to the road. The trucks had moved up and turned left at a fork. I was about the last one to get there. Everything was going good: jeeps and trucks and tanks and GIs everywhere were getting reassembled. Lt. Sabin told me to stay behind and be sure I Company found their trucks, and then come back. So I trotted back to look for any of the boys.

I started past a jeep and there lying on a stretcher on the back seat was Lt. Colonel Shelor, commander of the 3rd Battalion. His green fatigue coveralls were spattered with mud, and he lay on his back with his right hand over his forehead. His helmet was off and his face seemed very white. His driver, T/5 Perkins, was leaning against the jeep face first with his helmet off. "Hey, Perkins," I said, "what happened? Hey—hey?"

He stood up and looked at me: "What is it?"

"Are you alright, man?" I asked.

"Yeah . . . we were at the head of the column when the colonel suddenly pointed up and said: 'My God, I see a bazooka shell!' It came down on us like a mortar shell and landed under the front of the jeep. It blew us into the ditch. Colonel Shelor is in shock—bruised up a little . . . I've got a terrible headache and hurt all over, but otherwise we're OK—guess we got off easy at that."

"You got help comin'?" I asked.

"Yeah . . . yeah . . . Gowan: we'll be OK."

Whenever we came to villages the tanks were there first and often they were shooting and we would see clouds of smoke rising up to darken the white buildings. And all along the road German soldiers who had quit came down the road at a trot with their hands clasped behind their heads.

Along one lonely stretch of the road, we stopped. There was a house behind us and a house off to our right front. We watched the two houses and the fields. The windows in the houses were dead black, the wind blew across the grass, rippling it and bending it back in an unending blowing. Up the road in the other trucks we heard laughing. We looked up the road and saw a single Kraut in his drawers running down the road towards us. Three other Krauts came running down the road. They were stopped a couple of times up the line by GIs who searched them. When they got to our truck, two GIs were prepared to do it again. The rest of us tried to persuade them not to. They couldn't possibly have had anything left, but they searched them anyway, and then motioned them on summarily. When we pulled away from there I looked back and a half dozen German soldiers crawled out of the ditch opposite where our truck had been stopped and began running down the road.

Ahead lay a large community. A road sign said this was Modena. From the first moment we entered the main street, pandemonium of the craziest sort let loose. The street was full of men, women and children. What were we—had we become larger than life? Were we truly liberators? Or, more to the fact, had not the Germans just quit fighting and were running back home at last? We did not know. We rolled in to the center of Modena and stopped. Confusion then, bubbling, hysterical voices, crying, laughing—all at once. Women came running with loaves of bread and bottles of wine. In no time the rear end of the truck was piled high. We put all the bottles we could under the seats to keep them from tipping over.

Down the street a band of teenagers went slightly crazy and began firing into the air. Instantly, Sabin was up, barking at the populace, the rest of us on the truck pointed at them too; beseeching their elders to stop the kids from shooting their captured German guns. We didn't want anyone to get hurt. I saw a pair of shoes on the floor of the truck. They were smooth to the touch, blonde colored, with a thin leather sole, and were cut low, almost like carpet slippers. I picked them up and held them up to my combat boots. It was close enough. I quickly took off my combat boots and slipped on the streamlined Italian shoes. Sabin had sat down on the truck seat again. He looked dazed by all the excitement and did not seem to notice what I was doing. I threw my combat boots away and rejoiced in the svelte new footwear this wonderful day had brought me. The women pressing close to the truck knew that Sabin was our leader. They were pushing bread and wine at him, calling him a brave American lieutenant. One woman saw him bending over and put her arms around his neck and kissed him. Lt. Sabin blushed gloriously and smiled greatly as he lifted her arms from his neck. The bread piled ever higher, so we tried to give some of it back, and refuse any more. But they laughed and screamed at us and threw the bread over our heads into the truck. One woman brought us a sweet nut cake and we each had a bite. I nudged Gruenwald, who was sitting beside me: "Jerry, look over there—in that doorway." He nodded. "Isn't she pretty? The black-haired one looking this way. She's so happy she's helpless."

Gruenwald and I watched her. She stood in a doorway and the tears rolled down her cheeks. She was speechless. It was beautiful.

Everyone was pouring out wine and handing it up. I had to accept it, I had to drink it. As I drank I saw some women giving us water.

116

Then the trucks moved and we went to the other end of Modena. Here it was the same. The people around us were very emotional. Some had American flags, but the men mostly wore the Allied bands on their arms. Some women gave us bouquets of flowers and some women threw them at us. One woman ran over to her lilac bush full of white blossoms and hacked off a big branch with a butcher knife and brought them to me. I thanked her and then stood up and raised the thick white blossoms high over my head.

The trucks rolled again. We left Modena quickly and found we were not tired, nor hungry. We were all intoxicated by our success in war. There was wine enough for all, and bread, and a little water. Ours was now a triumphant, joyous procession. Now we were liberators. To hell with the voice of the road: it dealt only with the unfortunate ones, the losers in the game of war. That low, weary voice would bother me no more. I wasn't hoofing it today: no, I was rolling along as sweet as you please.

Now the dash was on for the Po. We sped northward across the Po Valley, through the towns of Capri and Guastalla. Then we were near the Po River. The trucks slowed and then stopped. Our joyous ride was over. The Po was an unknown risk at that point. So the trucks had to turn back. The tanks, too, could go no farther. We were dumped out on the road and told to be quiet. The wind was still blowing across the brightly greening fields. I heard a skylark as it soared above the convoy. God, I thought, how unfair it is to hear this bird again; how cruel to watch it climb up into the sky and disappear among the clouds that come to settle on the river and await the morning sun.

We marched slowly; the Po was not far now, but it was too late in the day to attempt a crossing. The

117

light of day slowly faded. We came to a village and then to the ruins of a large cathedral. We were told to find resting places around the ruins and to eat cold C rations quietly and then turn in because we were very near the Po and the crossing would take place on the morrow.

I nestled beside a broken statue. It had been a heroic figure when the cathedral rested serenely on its crossbeams and mighty arches. It seemed to have grown from the soil I lay on. Its severed arms gestured upward at—at what?—perhaps at the vision of a cross in the nave. Its head, large and unkempt in appearance, was tipped back, worshiping with sightless eyes the invisible figure of Jesus Christ nailed to his cross. I spread my gear close about me and settled back on my raincoat and looked up the statue gesturing futilely at the sky. I knew Easter was near: or had it passed already? Oh well, what the hell difference did it make anyway? So Jesus Christ was resurrected from his tomb and rose again briefly alive and then entered his Father's Kingdom. I had heard the story from the time of my childhood.

A large bat darted out from the ruins and then swooped low over my head. I thought I heard it chattering softly at me as I knew it did to its nestmates during the long daylight hours.

I watched a great star sink ever so slowly toward the western horizon. I analyzed the pathetic statue: what had its worship brought it or its sculptor except a long slow decay, then mutilation, then abandonment by the very people it was created for.

"So, anyway, God, I know you are up there," I said softly, "and I know you see me and that you hear me, and I know you believe me: but I do not believe you really care about us. There have always been wars, and the Bible says there will always be wars. So, God, I ask you: do I really need to be forgiven?"

The bat flew in and out of the ruins. It squeaked so softly that I knew only God could hear it. I drifted off to sleep and wondered why God had not made me in the likeness of a skylark.

April 23, 1945

Holman tapped my feet and jarred me awake.

"Eat a C ration and be ready to move out on a moment's notice."

The first orange rays of sunlight were penetrating into the ruins as I sat up and peeled the lid off a cold can of ham and eggs. I looked down at the food. I was hungry, but it did not look very good. I took a deep breath and held it while I put the first spoonful of food in my mouth. I had to swallow it with water in order to keep from gagging. I looked around and saw GIs sitting up throughout the ruins eating their C rations. A lieutenant from another company came through, followed by a very distraught sergeant.

"Lieutenant, sir," he said in a despairing voice, "we cannot put these men in rowboats and expect them to make it across without heavy casualties." The lieutenant was not listening to him and kept on walking.

The sergeant broke into tears and wailed loudly: "But, sir, I cannot send my men to their certain deaths. The Krauts will have their machine guns waiting, and they will lower their 88 batteries and shoot them flat across the river like giant rifles! I say I will not lead my men"—he stopped to weep openly and then ran to catch up with the lieutenant. I continued

121

to hear him crying and carrying on as they disappeared from sight among the ruins now half bathed in the light from the slowly rising sun. I had never seen a GI break down before like that. It gave me the willies. Of course, he could not go on. The crossing of the Po he would not be able to participate in. My mental condition was good. I knew sitting there that I would obey the order to move out, no matter how black the situation. I was having an adventure beyond my wildest imaginings. Now Holman came in view.

"Come on John T., Luhaink, Crest, Rebel—all of you—you have a lot to do." We threw on our gear and followed Holman out from the shadows of the ruins into full sunlight.

There before us was the Po River, a gentle winding little river that was now our Rubicon. How fitting, I thought suddenly. Caesar had not hesitated 2000 years before to cross the little Rubicon River in order to march on Pompey and Rome. We would cross our Rubicon and march north and, if need be, march on Hitler and Berlin. The river shore was sandy and I saw at least two dozen large "rowboats." The river was peaceful. I saw no sign of trouble on the far shore and no weapon was being fired within our earshot.

"Come on, come on—move it—get in this boat." Lt. Sabin was exhorting us. Two squads of us climbed into the boat and sat down quietly and quickly. A sergeant sat in the prow and told us to pick up the oars. We were given a good push by some Italian partisans and out we floated into the current. I helped row and noticed many other boats near us making the crossing. The silence was eerie. We rowed with all our might and soon were across on the beach without incident. As we formed up and moved off the beach, an old Italian man ran towards us from his house.

"Tedeschi tutta via!" he yelled at us over and over, pointing to the north. We knew what he was saying: "Germans all gone." The tension eased as we watched the old man dance around in circles.

When all the boats had crossed, Captain Bucher and Lt. Sabin sorted out the platoons, counted the men, and then led us off the beach and headed north once again. I looked back several times at the disappearing Po. I thought of the despairing sergeant who had broken up over what he conceived lay just ahead of him. One crisis too many it was for him, I thought. What heroic act had he performed on Mt. Belvedere? I mused. What had he done on a night patrol into no-man's land on a dark, dark night? Had he thrown a hand grenade and wiped out a machine gun nest that no one else would tackle? Was he like Sabin or Carafa—an instinctive hero—who had had one challenge handed him more than he could tolerate? Then I remembered little Private Brown from the steel mills of Pennsylvania. He had not been able to tolerate his first crisis. But he was not to be pitied. No, a man who cannot kill another human being is not to be pitied. So I was no longer angry with him. I shook it off and gave my attention once again to the column and the countryside and to the road.

The day was young and we were young and the Germans were running. There was a lilt in our step as we headed ever north from the Po. In the early afternoon we began to run into reception committees . . . a whole family at a time. They brought chairs and stools from their homes and set them straight along our line of march. Pails of wine and water were placed there for us to use. As we went by, we grabbed a glass and gulped it down and then ran to catch up

123

with the column. Again I looked back and saw almost every GI doing the same.

Sabin was not a drinker. I think he disapproved of our drinking wine as we marched. I watched him a little. He held his head high and pretended not to see the wine. Field after field—it went on and on—family after family of Italians offering us wine and water. Then we saw bread. A little boy or girl would come running out of their home and give us a piece of bread as we passed by. We began to feel good. The long march from the Po became more and more bearable. I heard laughter up and down the column. All my pockets were full of bread and I ate it as fast as I could. A little girl stood in the field holding two loaves of bread. I left the column and took one from her.

"Grazie—grazie!" I yelled back at her as I ran to rejoin the column. The wine, the wonderful wine was working on us now, changing our perceptions, making our day in the Italian countryside very pleasant indeed. All the women who came out to greet us looked very happy—many were crying. One old woman ran after us laughing, crying and raving. We dismissed her as a screaming old fool; but I was overwrought too.

Now there was no mournful voice of the road to haunt me. Now our feet made a new sound: A hup two three four! A hup! and a hup! and a hup two three four! There was a racy beat and a sweet rhythm to the sound.

A click and a clack and a clickity clack clack! My Italian shoes with their thin leather soles were skipping along the road. The wine made me tipsy—just tipsy enough to see and hear and feel: by God but it was good to be alive!

We stopped and sat down under a row of trees. It

was now late afternoon. Three small girls ran out of a house. They were pretty. They sat down under a tree and began to play. They seemed oblivious to our presence.

Then we were off and running again. We stopped infrequently, and now we drank water instead of wine. It grew dark and our rapid pace slowed a bit. I finally began to limp. My fine Italian shoes had sharp edges and they were beginning to cut my feet. The moon came up and still we marched. I was limping badly now. I cursed my impulsiveness. It was close to midnight when we stopped and invited ourselves into a group of houses beside the road. Several of us went up a dark stairway and collapsed on a bare floor.

April 24, 1945

A DAY OF REST FOR I COMPANY. I ROLLED ABOUT ON the floor and dreamed and slept fitfully. Daylight invaded the room and kept waking me up. But none of us rose until late afternoon when hunger got us up. Sabin and Bucher dined on freshly cooked noodles downstairs in the kitchen. I crept down the stairs a little and watched them eat. Damn! but it looked good! I went on outside and opened up a cold can of spaghetti and meat balls and pretended I was in an Italian restaurant and ate and gagged on most of it until my imagination ran out. I slunk back up the stairs and stretched out on the floor again, and was soon asleep.

April 25, 1945

THE SUN WAS ALREADY UP, FLOODING THE BARE room with orange light, when I awoke, hungry. I stepped over my sleeping comrades and ventured cautiously down the stairs. An old, old woman with a white shawl over her head and shoulders looked up at me and smiled and beckoned for me to follow her. We went into the kitchen. She pointed at a plate on the long wooden table and nodded her head at me. I took my helmet off and put it on the floor and sat down on a bench. The woman took my plate to the stove and filled it with hot noodles, poured an oily dressing over it, and then sprinkled little bits of green parsley over it all. She brought it to me and, smiling a toothless smile and nodding, she set it in front of me.

"Grazie—grazie, signora," I said, gratefully. She nodded some more and backed out of the kitchen and left me alone. There was just the plate: no eating utensils, so I pulled out my mess kit spoon and devoured the noodles in a hurry. As I left the house, the old woman grinned at me from the corner and nodded and waved a little. I grinned back and went outside to look for a pair of combat boots. Some jeeps had arrived in the night. In the back of one I found a small pile of GI uniforms and well-used boots. A GI came up to me.

"What're you lookin' for, soldier?" I saw he was the driver.

"Uh, I lost my boots in Modena, and these Wop shoes are killing my feet. Do those boots belong to anybody?"

"Not anymore. An ambulance crew gave us these clothes yesterday. Go ahead, try on some boots." The first pair fit perfectly. The leather felt soft and reassuring. I threw the Wop shoes out in the orchard. I saw Holman running around, and Sabin, gathering up the platoon. It was time to go again. A quick C ration for most—none for me—and we were off. Our spirits were still high after the long rest. My feet were happy once more and my pack seemed light. During the long day's march, we passed by Mantua to the west and Villafranca, also to the west. By nightfall we were at the southern shore of Lake Garda. The Germans obviously were in full retreat. We had heard no gun fire all day. At Lake Garda we found a good paved road that bordered the lake. We plodded along wearily in and out of tunnels, past several abandoned 88mm batteries with their long barrels pointing south, lowered for point blank firing against our tanks. We finally stopped and climbed above the road and spread out in some elegant gardens for the night.

"Hey, Luca," I said, "you heard anything?"

"About what?"

"About where we're going?"

"Nope. Have you?"

"No—I just hope it ends soon."

"Me too. Go to sleep, Bass."

April 26, 1945

AT DAYBREAK WE WERE AWAKENED BY HOLMAN.

"Come on, John T., Luhaink, Rebel, You, Fronk—come on—get up—we're headed for Riva."

Now, as we neared the shadows of the Dolomite Alps to the north, the weather changed. A vast gray cloud mass drifted over us from the Alps and dampened our victorious march. Then a light drizzle came down. We marched swiftly, looking down at Garda, at exquisite villas and lavish gardens.

"Holman!" I yelled, "how far to Riva?" He shook his head and did not answer. At noon, we rested and ate a K ration. Lake Garda had turned gray and the drizzle still came down, so that we were wet—lightly wet. The afternoon grew darker and then we began to see the end of the lake. It came to a point in the distance and the foothills of the Alps rose behind it. Then we saw the village of Riva. It was nearly dark. The village was also dark. It was a dismal sight, and I had a sinking feeling in my heart. What lay beyond Riva? The Dolomites looked black and ominous. I knew the German Army was up there: They could defend the mountain passes indefinitely. . . .

131

No hup hup hup now—but a shuffling sound.
Not a laugh and a shout—but a very long look at
  Riva.
The Alps, my boys, are calling!
We will yodel tomorrow, my boys, from the
  heights!
We will pick the edelweiss—we will cross the great
  white glacier.
We will climb the Alps, my boys!
Oh leo ladie! O ladie—oh ladie hoo!

We swung into Riva in the dark. There was no one on the street. No wine, no flowers, no bread—not even water—we were just another army coming in and occupying, taking charge, giving orders, looking for women and wine. The rules would change very little. The Germans were not far away now. The villagers trembled in their homes: a new army was here—what would there be new for them to fear?

Our squad was lucky: on the west outskirts of Riva, we found two-story, deserted but furnished houses. The Germans had been there before us. But they left in a hurry and so we ate their food and slept on their comfortable cots.

April 27, 1945

WE WERE ALLOWED TO WALK INTO RIVA BUT WERE told to return for evening chow. Luca and I strolled into town, but stayed, as instructed, on the main street that ran along the lake shore. There were few people on the street. It was a cool, gray day. Some GIs rented rowboats and rowed about, in violation of Captain Bucher's orders. We watched them getting drunk in the boats, and then walked around the point to the edge of Riva. We stopped and looked north—up at the mighty Alps.

"They're up there," I said to Luca. "They're waiting for us to come."

"I heard a rumor today, Bass—I think it's true."

"What—what did you hear?"

"I heard we may be issued winter gear so we can climb those mountains and fight the Krauts again." I had no comeback. I was stunned into silence. Slowly we made our way back through Riva to the house. In the kitchen we found some flour, so I made some crazy kind of batter, using water, and made pancakes for the squad.

April 28–May 1, 1945

Nothing of interest to write about.

May 2, 1945

DEAR MOM AND DAD:

I am writing this to you late in the day. It has been a truly wonderful day. Earlier, I was out on the lake in a rowboat with my buddy, Luca, when all of a sudden we heard several guns being fired from the shore, near the village. We didn't know what was going on, so we fell down flat in the boat and waited. Well, the shooting kept up and so we got up and looked around. There were people running along the shore and shooting their guns in the air. We even heard bullets hit the water near us. We knew something was up, so we rowed to shore and stopped the first GI we saw. "What is it? What is all the shooting for?" This GI was looking very wild: "What is it?" he yelled. "What is it? It is over—the war is over!!" Anyway, the men in this village shot their rifles over the lake all afternoon and tonight there is a big victory celebration going on in the middle of town. I know you are as happy as I am. I can't wait now until we return to the States. More later.

Love, John T.

May 3, 1945

HOLMAN CAME TO EACH ROOM AND WOKE US UP. AS I went through the hall to the kitchen, I saw Holman and Sgt. Gruenwald trying to wake up a young GI sleeping on a cot in the hall. He was new to the outfit—fresh out of the reppo-deppo in Rome. I slowed up and then stopped to watch.

"Come on, Smith," Holman said, shaking him by his shoulder, "the celebration is over."

"Wait, John!" Gruenwald said, "I don't like the way he looks. Let's take his pulse." They both took his pulse. Holman straightened up and looked at us. "He won't be getting up." We stared at the still figure.

"Where was he last night?" Holman asked the squad.

"He was with us, and returned with us," someone said.

"What was he drinking?"

"We each had a bottle of champagne. But later, Smith bought himself a bottle of red wine and drank that too."

"Maybe his bottle was poisoned," Gruenwald ventured. Holman covered Smith with his blanket.

"I'll find Captain Bucher and the medics. The rest of you go in the kitchen and try to eat something."

We nodded silently and filed into the kitchen. Nothing looked good, so we drank some coffee. Presently we heard Bucher, Holman, and the medics come in. Nobody moved while they carried Smith out.

"Well—well, that's that," Rebel said softly to himself.

"I wonder who hated us last night? Everyone was laughing and dancing and crying," Ruppert said.

"Who knows?" Fronk said. "The Krauts lived in this town a long Goddamned time."

"It's the shits," Luhaink said, "Smith never even was in a battle—never fired his M1." A melancholy silence settled on us. Later in the day, I felt the urge to play the piano. We had found a battered grand piano in the living room. I went down and looked around the room. At one time, it had been handsomely furnished. On one side, large windows afforded a view of Lake Garda. A large sofa and several chairs had been slashed and broken apart. A once red and blue, expensive rug lay in filthy pieces beyond the piano which had suffered heavy damage also. I stood at the keyboard and tried to create some chords with my left hand. It was useless: only jingling, bizarre sounds came forth. I left the room in a black mood and did not go near it again.

Night fell. I walked to the lake. A cold breeze swept from the Alps and whined across the lake. My helmet was in the house. I shivered as the cold air pushed through my hair. Down the shore, in Riva, the villagers and our GIs were celebrating the end of the war again. Accordion music came across the lake. I heard shouting and laughter, and several shots. I returned to the house and crawled into my cot: sobered by Smith's death, but grateful that the war, which claimed him mysteriously at the end, had spared me.

May 4, 1945

"COME ON, JOHN T.; WAKE UP." IT WAS HOLMAN, at the ungodly hour of 6:00 A.M.

"Why? What's up?" I asked.

"We're going out on a hike, weapon nomenclature, the usual training routine. It's to keep us from going soft." I groaned and rolled over, but I kept my eye on Holman, and when he returned with a slender board in his hand, I jumped quickly off the cot.

Outside, on the street, I saw that it promised to be a fair spring day. We hiked casually, almost gaily, although in formation, out of Riva and then turned off a dirt path that led up a steep wooded hillside. After a mile we left the path and spread out over a grassy slope, each platoon occupying its own separate ground for the purpose of the training exercise. Then the squads formed into separate units, sitting in little semicircles on the ground, looking down at the exercise leaders a few feet below them. Holman put a blanket on the ground below us and asked Crest to take apart his BAR, name each part and explain how it worked, and then reassemble it. Crest did the routine in his low, calm voice.

Without warning a burst of gunfire erupted violently from the area of our neighboring squad to the left, followed by terrible screams and shouting. Automatically, without thinking, I rolled over on my stomach and pointed my M1 down the slope. Some of the squad lay with me on their stomachs; the rest ran up the hill. The screaming, a high-pitched, terrifying sound, continued for a few more seconds. There was no further gunfire. I looked over at the GIs running around like crazy men and I realized that the firing somehow had happened within the squad. Then, out of the milling frenzied group, Cross came limping towards me.

"You're bleeding, Cross," I gasped, scrambling to my feet. "What happened? Were you hit?"

"Yes—yes—God—yes, I was hit in the leg, but I've got a tourniquet—I can walk—won't wait for medics—God—how awful for this to happen." He limped past me toward the path. I now realized that the screaming had stopped. I looked around wildly: GIs were still shouting—still running about. No one took charge. We were like a flock of disoriented, devastated sheep. I spied Rabideau coming towards me. Blood was dripping from his left hand.

"Here—wait, Rabideau!" I cried. I pulled out an unused handkerchief from my pocket. "Let me tie this around your hand. Is that your only wound?"

"Yeah, Bass, I was lucky. I only got one round right through the middle of my hand."

"What happened?" I asked as I walked with him toward the path. "Was it your BAR that fired?"

"Yeah. I saw it happen. Hackett took it apart, and when he had it put back together, it was pointed uphill at us, on the bipod. I think he was half asleep, like the rest of us. When it was finished, I heard him say, 'Now the last thing you do is pull the trigger.' "

"Who was screaming?"

"Schuck. He got two bullets just below his neck."

"Is he dead?"

"Don't know. Thanks for the 'kerchief—see you later." I ran back to the slope to find my squad. I discovered them throwing their ammunition away, into the bushes. Rebel was crying.

"Come on, Bass, throw your bullets away. Schuck may be dead. My prayers for a peaceful, good end to this conflict have not been heard. No—instead—he may have been killed by a friend—a comrade! Throw your bullets far away, Bass, so this cannot happen again." I threw the loaded clip in my M1 away. I saw Holman doing the same as the others.

"Where is Schuck?" I asked Holman.

"They carried him down the path."

"Is it alright if I return to the house?"

"Yes." I walked to the path and started down. Most of the company had preceded me. I wanted to run, but something held me back. An unmistakable trail of blood showed me where the three GIs had gone. Down on the lake road I saw an ambulance sitting unattended across the road in front of some buildings. I was still alone. The road was deserted. I saw that the rear doors of the ambulance were open. I walked slowly across the road and stopped at the doors. There, lying on his back, feet-first in the ambulance, was Schuck. He was naked from the waist up, his eyes were closed, he was unconscious. I looked below his chin and saw two perfectly round bullet holes just below his collar bone. They had been neatly dusted with sulfa powder. What was happening? I saw no one. I heard nothing. There was only poor Schuck lying there, probably dead, and me. There was no hint of terror, or suffering, on his face. He was young, like me. I could not look at him any longer. I turned and walked back to Riva.

Later that day, I ran across Hackett. We did not speak. His face was as white as snow. He was nervous and he looked wary. For Hackett, as for Schuck, Cross and Rabideau, the war had ended, but then, like the most horrible of all nightmares, it had begun again.

June 1945

WE MOVED TO CIVIDALE, IN THE NORTHEAST COR-
ner of the Po Valley, to await the order to return to
the States.

An opportunity came to go mountain climbing in
Austria. I was tired of drinking champagne and writing letters, so I said I'd go. Thirty of us set out early one morning in three troop trucks and began the
long climb on narrow, winding roads into the Carnic
Alps.

> The Alps, my boys, are calling!
> We will yodel tomorrow, my boys,
> From the heights!
> We'll pick the edelweiss,
> We'll cross the great white glacier,
> We'll climb the Alps, my boys!
> Oh leo ladie! O ladie! Oh ladie hoo!

From Cividale to Gemona, from Gemona to Heiligenblut, from Heiligenblut to Lienz. As we climbed
ever higher, the rank, humid air of the Po Valley vanished and we grew cool as the trucks brought us into
the crystal clear mountain air. Beyond Lienz, the road
climbed sharply upward, then leveled briefly to bring
us to three simple, wooden barracks.

"OK, men," Sgt. Penny announced, "We're here. This is Mount Grossglockner, and I'm told the Grossglockner glacier is right over there behind that ridge. Find yourselves bunks. Sorry, but your K and C rations will have to feed you on this trip. The weather is good, and the climb for tomorrow looks very promising."

We were at an altitude of nine or ten thousand feet. I was a little light-headed, so I crawled into the first bunk inside the door and lay down. The sun was already behind the mountain, and day was turning swiftly into night. Luhaink climbed into the bunk above me and bounced on the boards, threatening to collapse the bed. The other GIs were subdued. The thin air had us all moving in slow motion. We ate a cold C ration. There was no electricity, so we turned in as the last light of the sunset faded. The plain board bunks were uncomfortable. I grew cold, and slept little.

Sgt. Penny came in at 7:00 A.M. and woke us up. "OK, men, I want you to have a good time today. You have a choice: you can climb on your own, or you can join us. I'm leading a climb to the top of Grossglockner." Luca and I and four others elected to go where we pleased. We ate our cold C rations and were ready. The sun had already flooded the narrow valley below us with light. As we left the barracks, I stopped and looked up the mountain. Sgt. Penny was leading a sizable group of GIs. He was taking one measured step after another: not fast—not slow—just steady. He was using his ice axe as a walking aid. His expression was solemn. Penny was a natural born mountain man.

"Come on, Bass," Luca said, "Let's go find that glacier." A trail led over the ridge and then we looked down at the glacier. To our front, the glacier ended and the melting ice water ran out of it and became a little stream. To our right front, the glacier filled the gap between Grossglockner and a smaller mountain. Then it stretched way off to our right, white and massive, and became part of the snowy Carnic Alps.

We had brought our ice axes. We jumped and ran down to the glacier. The air became noticeably cooler. Then we slid down a muddy slope and ran out on the glacier.

"Hey, Bass: there's snow on the far side. Let's go sliding." We came to a crevasse.

"Luca, it's only six feet wide: I'll jump across." I backed up, and holding the ice axe out in front of me, I ran a few steps and just made it to the top edge on the other side. I deliberately fell forward and plunged the blade deep into the glacier. It held me though my lower body did not quite reach the top of the surface. I was not cold, but a long cold invisible cloud of ice air reached up out of the crevasse and enticed me to slide down, to give up my little struggle and succumb and slip down into the blue and white depths, to rest—for once and for all—to rest.

Luca yelled at me. "I don't like that Bass," he said. "I'm going around that big hole. Come on, get your ass out of that hole!"

I woke up and pulled on the ice axe and left the crevasse behind . . . We climbed up a steep snow slope across the glacier and then sat down and slid down on our behinds. The white ice was blinding in the sunlight.

As night fell, on February 19, 1945, we were told to gather up our gear. We marched down the ancient bricked street of Prunetta to our waiting trucks. The usual shouting of orders was absent. All orders were given just above a whisper. We rolled down the winding road from Prunetta. I watched the long column of trucks behind us, headlights shooting out in every direction. There was no small talk in the truck. We all knew where we were going:

It's off to war we go, my lads,
To fight the bloody Hun!

We'll not come back, you can be sure
Until the job is done.

We'll drink and dance and sing tonight
Before the dawn dare break.

And then—
It's off to war we go, my lads,
Until the war is won!

And then we started up again.

As I watched, suddenly, all the headlights of the convoy were shut off. We slowed to a crawl as we wound steadily up the mountain road. Then it was over: the long prelude to war was over. Again, orders were whispered to us. We were to be very quiet. We formed up and moved out up the same winding road. A dark massive mountain became dimly visible. We left the road and wound ever higher up a trail that ended in a scrubby stand of pines at the base of the mountain. We had two hours to kill. The assault on Belvedere would begin at 11:30 P.M. sharp. I found a soft spot under a tree and fell over on my side, but discarded nothing. I tried not to think about it: I tried to concentrate on where Holman was because I did not want to lose him. I wasn't hungry, but I was thirsty. I drank a little from my canteen. The mountain above us was very peaceful. Perhaps, I thought vacantly, the Germans are gone.

Then it was time. Holman came through the trees and whispered: "On your feet, John T.—This is it."

I followed him and saw the rest of my squad do likewise. Then I saw the entire company, I Company, converge around me and we all followed our squad leaders through the trees. The angle of ascent took a sharp turn upward. We ran into large clumps of bushes and stopped. My old buddy, John Breu, could speak German fluently. Someone had the bright idea that he should yell up the mountain at the Germans—that he should yell: "Surrender!" So he grabbed onto some bushes, tipped back his head and shouted the word in German. His yell brought an instant reaction: several burp guns were fired at us from above, but were aimed too high and no one was hit.

The foolishness over with, now the climb began in earnest. From this point on, overwhelmed and made numb by fear, I found that I obeyed all orders mechanically and reacted to the movements of men in front and behind me in the same way. It never occurred to me to collapse, to sit down and freeze, to cry, to run, to scream. I had never done any of these things before so I quietly moved off the trail at one point, managed to pull down my trousers, and relieved my bowels instead. I found I was not alone in this. Among the bushes we passed Sergeant Gruenwald, sitting helplessly by the trail, left behind by his squad. Earlier, about 10:00 P.M., I saw Jordan, a veteran bar room brawler, become sick, and then stumble and fall out of the line of march into the ditch.

Burp guns chattered overhead. German artillery fired 88 shells that could not find the high narrow ridge, and so we were lucky, we survived. I crept ever upward—one in a line of creeping men who wanted to capture a mountain.

At sunrise, two young German soldiers crawled out of a cave and surrendered. Two watches were taken from them. I came upon the scene. My buddy, John Breu, was there. The soldiers had been students at Heidelberg. The watches were special prizes for academic achievement. They protested to Breu and asked for their watches back. Breu's face was red: he was upset. I knew at once that he was on their side. He was of German descent. When we had finished basic training at Camp Blanding, Florida, we knew we were going overseas to fight the Nazis. Breu, who loved his German ancestry dearly, went into the CO one day and spoke to the captain of our company: "Captain," he said, "I'll go to Europe to fight for our country, but I want to make one thing clear: in combat, I will not shoot a German soldier unless I know he is aiming to kill me first." This interview did not get him in trouble. And he served well until the end of the war.

The prisoners did not get their watches back. They were sent to the rear, unescorted, their hands clasped over their black helmets.

Suddenly, bullets whined about us and ripped through our fatigues. We scraped frantically at the mountain with our steel helmets until we had small depressions carved out into which we only half fit. But we had gained the summit of Mt. Belvedere. We held fast, and the Germans retreated.

"Let's get off this thing and climb that mountain," Jones said. We left the glacier and started up Grossglockner. The trail was steep, but not difficult. Then a fork appeared. Luhaink and the others decided to explore the unknown trail. I looked up the visible trail and decided to continue on it, alone. I was getting tired, and my trail looked safe—I could see no surprise in it. I climbed steadily for an hour and a half. Then I saw a little path that branched off the main trail and led to a look-out point. I needed a break, so I took the little path to its end, a steep, grassy nook. I stopped there and looked down. I was instantly dizzy and sat down. Beyond the little grassy nook there was only air. Straight down below me I saw some cabins that were no bigger than little match sticks. Then I heard voices. I looked behind me. No one was there. I peeked over the edge of the nook and saw Jones's ski cap, and then his red face, covered with sweat.

"What luck," I cried, "we meet again." Jones was very unhappy. He was an expert rock climber, but I could see he was flustered.

"Bass," he panted, as he searched for hand holds just below the nook, "I won't do this again. I don't know what happened—but it was not a good climb today." We remembered each other from that morning on top of Mt. Belvedere when the remaining Krauts were shooting at us. He was wounded and staggered over to me.

"I'm hit in the leg, Bass—what'll I do?"

"Jones," I said, "take my sulfa tablets and canteen and head back down the mountain for help. There are no medics up here." He protested, but I thrust them into his hands, and he left. Now, fully recovered, he could not enjoy a precipitous, dangerous climb. He pulled himself over the edge into the nook and fell on his stomach, clutching at the grass and breathing hard. Close behind him came Luca Luhaink. He looked happy and confident.

"Luca," I cried, "how did it go?"

"I eat this shit up," he said.

The climb was over. Jones slowly recovered his composure, and drank some water, and did not look out and down at the view.

"It's getting late," Jones said. He crawled up to the path and was gone. Luhaink and the others left. I was last. As I returned to the main trail, I remembered about the flower, the flower of Switzerland, a little white, woolly-looking herb named edelweiss. I turned up off the trail and wandered through clumps of boulders and outcroppings of rocks. I went carefully along the slope, and then I saw a white cluster of unexciting flowers growing beside some boulders. I knelt down beside them. They were round and white with woolly petals. I picked two perfect flowers and put them in my shirt pocket. For me, also, the climb was over. I ran down the trail without stopping.

September 1945, Camp Swift, Texas
March 1988, Napa, California